"This book grew from the author's national empirical study of Catholic young people who said 'Preaching Matters.' How to make preaching better is about 'connecting.' Whether pew-sitter or preacher, read and share this book if you want to open the conversation about how important preaching is to the spiritual life of your community."

— Fred A. Baumer, Adjunct Professor of Preaching
St. John's School of Theology
Collegeville, Minnesota

"With her passionate desire to connect pulpits with pews, Bellinger opens the dialogue by interviewing countless parishioners young and old and by giving voice as well to Catholic priests and deacons. Doing so she provides the models and sets the pace for what needs to happen to bridge the gap between parishioner and preacher long before they enter their churches. Her academic research, together with her pastoral understanding, contributes well to her suggested directives inviting others to enter the dialogue that may produce Catholic preaching that is truly conversional."

— Msgr. James T. Telthorst, DMin
Archdiocese of St. Louis

"Bellinger has travelled the nation trying to crack the 'loud silence' that exists between Catholic preachers and their parishioners, with a special attentiveness to youth. In this book, she reports her discoveries, but perhaps even more important, she shows us how to continue the conversation in our own communities. The discussion questions posed at the end of the book are— alone—worth the price of the whole. They promise to provoke meaningful conversations at the local level that could substantially bolster the quality of preaching in the U.S."

—Ann M. Garrido, Associate Professor of Homiletics
Aquinas Institute of Theology

"Feel like there is a huge cavernous divide between the pulpit and the pew? If you want to close the gap, this is the book. It's historical and contemporary, it includes quantitative and qualitative research, you hear what preachers want and pew sitters desire. Gather a group of parishioners, share the questions in the back, become a listener who gives feedback, and feel the love grow. This is adult faith formation at its finest."

—Leland Nagel, Executive Director
National Conference ⌐ ⌐ ⌐ ⌐ ⌐ Leadership

Connecting Pulpit and Pew

Breaking Open the Conversation
about Catholic Preaching

Karla J. Bellinger

LITURGICAL PRESS
Collegeville, Minnesota

www.litpress.org

1	2	3	4	5	6	7	8	9

Library of Congress Cataloging-in-Publication Data

Bellinger, Karla.
    Connecting pulpit and pew : breaking open the conversation about Catholic preaching / Karla Bellinger.
        pages cm
    Includes bibliographical references.
    ISBN 978-0-8146-3769-2 — ISBN 978-0-8146-3794-4 (ebook)
    1. Preaching.   2. Catholic Church—Doctrines.   3. Catholic Church—United States—History—21st century.   I. Title.

BV4211.3.B365   2014
251.0088'282—dc23   2013050529

For Sophie and Samadhi,
who have blessed my life with joy.

Contents

Acknowledgments

God is good. Sunshine and warmth and the out-of-doors; the sandbox, the ravine, and the baseball field—my earliest memories are brightly lit and physically vital. God was there. God is here. My thankfulness rises from that foundation.

My life is full of people. So many have given me a leg up in life: my parents who raised a family of thinkers, my family who have supported me, washed the laundry and ate my oatmeal, and so many friends who have prayed for me and this work and asked for an update of "How is it going?" Thank you all.

As I began to research listening to listeners, the name of Ronald J. Allen popped up consistently. Ron responded promptly and graciously to each of my early questions and continues to support and further my explorations. Katherine Schmitt shared her prepublished insights into the NCEA study "Effective Preaching: What Catholics Want." During my doctoral coursework in preaching at Aquinas Institute, each of my professors furthered my understanding. Ann Garrido was the first to believe, letting me know that it was not crazy to be a mother of five, working full time, and pursuing a doctoral degree—if I was called to it, it would work out. At times I had reservations about that wisdom but, in the end, she was right. In his course Studying Congregations: Methods and Research, Fr. Mark A. Latcovich at St. Mary's Seminary persistently asked: "How do you measure 'connection'; how can you operationalize that?" My thinking sharpened as a result. William Baker of the University of Akron opened my eyes to see how psychological insights into listener receptivity could apply to preaching. Fr. Daniel Harris, CM, had a sense of humor and a meticulous eye that furthered the quality of my doctoral thesis, "Are you Talking to Me? A Study of Young Listeners' Connection with Catholic Sunday Preaching."

As he prepared to travel to Rome for the synod on evangelization in 2012, Archbishop Joseph Kurtz and I conversed about preaching, the "new evangelization," and youth. His encouragement has continued to spur me on.

In the spring of 2013, Bill Miller, Lee Nagel, and Joanie McKeown of the National Conference for Catechetical Leadership (NCCL) opened the doors for the "Catechesis in Preaching Research Initiative." Thus the voices of catechetical leaders joined with high school youth and clergy to enrich this study.

I am grateful to Bishop Richard G. Lennon for his episcopal blessing on me and my work. I am thankful for Mickey and Stephanie who have typed and transcribed. I am indebted to the theology teachers who made the paper survey happen as well as to so many who have shared with me their hopes and dreams for preaching. And though *Evangelii Gaudium* was released after I had submitted this manuscript for publication, I am grateful to Pope Francis for his fervor for the renewal of preaching. May this book further that vision through the words that follow.

PART ONE

The Search for Connection

When you click on your internet start page, a little circle goes round and round and round. The word "Connecting . . .," pops up next to the revolving circle. Suddenly, you are "connected" to every corner of the world. Do you want to buy a car? Do you want to chat with your classmates? Do you want to check if it will be sunny today? You can find that out in an instant. Remotely, your doctor can diagnose your diseases by looking at your data on her desktop. A student can graduate from an online university without ever dumping her backpack onto a chair in a classroom. You can read this as an e-book without ever turning a page. Connect . . . connect . . . connect. . . . You and I live in a connected world. It is no longer news. It is reality. "Connection" is our life.

By contrast, a Christian preacher physically walks to a pulpit or a stage. In a live performance, that man or woman speaks on behalf of God. The words cannot be edited or tidied up or rewound before they are sent out. There is no wireless router. There is no cell tower. There is no coaxial cable. How, then, is a preacher supposed to "connect"? Does the homiletical human bond matter anymore? Does preaching make a difference?

The Search for Connection

To Encounter God, Together

I ask not only on behalf of these, but also on behalf of those who will believe in me through their word, that they may all be one. As you, Father, are in me and I am in you, may they also be in us, so that the world may believe that you have sent me. (John 17:20-21)

"You Impact My Life"

We will call him "Michael."[1] When he took my survey, he was a freshman who went to a Catholic high school on the east coast of the United States. The question ran through my head as I flipped through his answers on my paper survey: does preaching make a difference to Michael? At fourteen, he has grown up in a generation accustomed to the internet. He likely listens to music through his ear buds. If he is like the others in his generation, dinner may be fast food in the car on the way to soccer practice or to his sister's ballet practice. I came to the question on page four, "Describe what happens when a person connects with you." He drew a picture of a cross surrounded by little hearts. Love and care, sharing and talking, praying and worshipping, hovered about that cross.

His other answers also exuded warmth. When asked to describe what it meant for a preacher to "connect" with him, Michael said, "For a preacher to connect with me, he must be able to see in the eyes of a kid/teenager. [D] is very good at communicating with kids as much as he does with adults."

At some point in the past year, that preaching has changed Michael's life. He penciled in what that transformation was like:

This experience was a huge impact on my life. I was so done with my terrifying experiences and going to Sunday homilies made me finally let it all go.

What experiences can be so "terrifying" so as to almost crush a four-teen-year-old boy? Escaping a house fire? Surviving a school shooting? Having recurring nightmares? He doesn't say. But he does describe the cause of his cure: "going to Sunday homilies made me finally let it all go."

My doctoral study of 561 young listeners asked why they came to Mass. Michael skipped past the boxes marked "To worship God," "To be entertained," "I was required to," or "To be with family and friends." He circled the last choice, "Other." Then on the blank line, he filled in why he was there: "to connect with God." His final comment, when asked to tell his preacher anything, was: "Thank you so much, [D]. You've been a great friend and [you] impact my life."

In this high-tech world, preaching *can* make a difference. It did for Michael. It still does all over the world. In the brilliant sunshine of Nigeria, a woman's heart burns within her as she nods and sways and claps her arthritic hands as her preacher shouts out the good news of Jesus Christ. In an ancient church on the edge of the square in a small town in France, a Brazilian priest tells a joke, and in their laughter, the choir senses how good it is to be together in that space. In the American South, a young woman slides across to her seat, wanting to share with her boyfriend the experience of the man whose sermons have changed her life. Every weekend, words of encouragement and challenge and exhortation pass from the mouths of preachers to people who seek to encounter the living God. The connection is real.

How does preaching make a difference? What makes a message connect so well that people want to shout it out to the whole world? And how can we help that to happen more often? I have been on a quest to find out.

The Search for Connection

In summer 2009, I visited my daughter in the foothills of the Sierra Nevada Mountains in California. She did not have room for me in her small house, so for three weeks I slept outside on the ground in a pop-up tent. Since my body was still on Eastern Time, each day I awoke at four o'clock in the morning with nothing to do in the silence and the darkness but to bask in the radiance of the stars and the moon—and pray. In the daytime, I was reading a popular book that asked, "What gives you life?" My internal response was what gives me life is connecting people with God—and its corollary, connecting people with each other. Where was I to go with that? I did not know.

I had begun my doctoral program in preaching with no clear idea of where it would lead. Yet I had felt strongly called to it, as a call that burned like an ember within me. What was I, a married Catholic lay-woman and mother, going to do with a doctorate in preaching? The call was not logical. Yet there it was: an unmistakable, irrational, smoldering compunction which would not go away even as I tried to make it go away. The first year of studies had passed. I had walked in with my hands open. Now what?

One dark morning in the second week of prayer, I awoke from a sound sleep with a powerful awareness. I sensed a sorrow and a grief at the disconnection within the people of God. I do not know if God mourns, but in that flash of insight, my heart ached, not unlike a mother who weeps over the conflicts of her adult children. Jesus prayed that we all be one (John 17:21). Jesus prayed that we all be one, and we are not.

My first thought was, "What can *I* do about that?" Following closely was the enormity of the rift accompanied by a feeling of profound small-ness as in "Who am I?" and "Whoa, wait a minute . . . , not me." In that moment in the tent in the Sierras, I sensed a response: I was in a unique position. As a convert to Catholicism, a mother, and a theologically-trained laywoman, I could offer a fresh voice from the pew for those in the pulpit; I could speak with a voice of love and hands for healing; I could listen to both sides so that we better understand each other. Trusting in the Holy Spirit, I could do what I could do to connect the pulpit and the pew, so that together we could grow closer to God. The first Eucharistic Prayer for Use in Masses for Various Needs expresses that vision more eloquently: "Strengthen the bond of unity between the faithful and the pastors of your people . . . that in a world torn by strife your people may shine forth as a prophetic sign of unity and concord." Fervor for this task took hold of me.

As a result, for the past four years, like a detective sifting through evidence, I have investigated "connection" in preaching. I have discussed this connection conundrum with anyone who would listen. I ran an empirical study of 561 Catholic high school students about how to connect with them in Sunday preaching.[2] I interviewed pastors. I surveyed catechetical leaders.[3] I observed listeners. I dug through the research in listening and in preaching. What did I find out?

A Taste of Hope

I learned that preaching is a deeply sensitive subject. I discovered that listeners hunger for inspiration; they want to hear a message that gives them life. Clergy told me that they thirst for their people to encounter Jesus Christ; they want to inspire their people; they want to see the fruit of a Christian life. I also heard undercurrents of frustration on both sides. I came across stories of great goodness, deep hurt, and rich transformation. Most of all, I discovered hope. It is out of that hope that I write this book.

There is good news: there are pockets where Catholic preaching is done well. Where there are difficulties, they are usually readily identifiable. There are people of good intent on both sides. There are concrete ways to strengthen what we have.

The encounter of preaching is complex. The improvement of preaching is challenging. Strengthening listeners to understand theological talk is an uphill climb. Complex, challenging, and an uphill climb, yes, but the task before us is not insurmountable. Difficult? Perhaps. Impossible? No. If we have the determination and the courage to take it on, we can pull together to create a culture of listening.

Change can happen. It begins with vision. We pray to the Holy Spirit to renew the church. What is our role in bringing about that renewal? Where do we concentrate our energies to create the most impact? To renew the church, we model after what we know of Jesus to strengthen our preaching. To revitalize our preaching, we open the conversation about the Sunday homily. To launch that interaction, we need a tool to help us to move forward together. The objective of this book is to be a springboard for that discussion.

This book also introduces fresh voices to the conversation in preaching: Young people tell us how to connect with them. Pastors talk of their experience of preaching. Lay leaders offer their insights. Listeners cry out for a gospel message that connects them, inspires them, and spurs them to spread the good news to the world in which they live. These are folks that the homiletics world has not heard from before.

At the same time, this book is not just written for students and professors in seminaries. This conversation is for anybody and for everybody—for those who care that the message of the gospel transforms us; for those who care that the grieving are comforted; for those who care that the light of Christ is brightly burning in a "whatever" age. The responsibility for an encounter with the God of love through the medium of preaching is not just borne by the one who delivers the message. Those who listen are also accountable.[4] As I was surrounded by charts and interview transcripts and correlations and graphs of responses, one piece of evidence stood out like a trumpet blast from a mountaintop. I call it "The Loud Silence."

The Loud Silence

Father [A] and I had talked for about an hour. We had squeezed our interview between the 7 a.m. Mass and his morning hospital visits. He grabbed his jacket and his granola bar and was dashing for the door when he turned and stopped. "Good luck," he said. "These are important questions [about preaching and connection]." He held the door open. "And," he looked at me with a puzzled look, "we never talk about it."

A fifteen-year-old boy in my survey wrote to his preacher: "Thank you, Father, for how you guide me to be more faith-filled. I like how you are comforting and always there to help. I can't thank you enough." He described how he had learned to pray as a result of his priest's preaching. As I read his comments, I thought to myself, "This is good stuff!" I flipped to an earlier page, to the question, "How often in fifty-two weeks do you give your preacher feedback (other than 'Good homily, Father')?" He had circled "Zero." The priest who had so impacted the lad's life had never heard a word about it.

As the consultant, I sat at the center of the U-shaped table in the meeting room. The leadership team had exuded about the people who chose to come to this parish in spite of having many other local options. I asked, "If you are looking to build upon your strengths, what is it that brings people to this particular place?" They radiated about the reverence of their liturgies, and then they were silent for a moment. "I think it's the preaching," said the man on my left in the green polo shirt. The others silently nodded. I turned to the elderly pastor who had founded the parish forty years earlier. "Father [B], do you get feedback on your preaching?" I asked. "No," he murmured and shook his head, "I never hear anything."

Before doing my research, I had always assumed that the scuttlebutt about preaching somehow found its way to the pulpit. Surely somebody talked to "them" about it. That is not necessarily the case. Though comments can travel at lightning speed across the parking lot and through cyberspace, few parishioners sit down over a cup of coffee with their homilist and discuss ways that he (or she, in the Protestant world) could help them to grow closer to God through the preaching. What has surprised me, as I have moved from swaying babies in the pew to sharing homiletical method with the theologically educated, is how much clergy *do not* hear these kinds of comments. In a focus group, I asked, "What kind of conversation about preaching is going on within the parishes?" One catechetical leader said, "There's no conversation. It's the elephant in the room. Everyone knows it's a big problem, but no one is willing to talk about it."

Clergy tell me they don't talk much about preaching among themselves either. It would be rare for a homilist to approach a group of parishioners to ask, "How can I help you to understand better?" or "How could my message lift you up? What would help to strengthen your commitment to your faith?" or "What most resonates for you (or doesn't) in my preaching?" This is not just a Catholic phenomenon. Lori Carrell, in *The Great American Sermon Survey,* found that only 9 percent of both Protestant and Catholic clergy got constructive feedback about their preaching (other than the random comment during the handshake at the door).[5]

Every tale worth telling contains a struggle. The "villain" in the "preaching story" is "The Loud Silence." There is little interaction. Collaboration is virtually nonexistent. There is almost no research.[6] How are we to know what is actually happening? We can suppose. We can make assumptions. Each person will work out of his or her experience. Preaching books are almost all written by those who preach. They may make "sender-side" assumptions about effectiveness (and listeners) which may or may not hold. People who listen may make "receiver-side" presumptions about preaching (and preachers) which may or may not be valid. We could each be mistaken. There is much that we do not see and even more that we do not know.

The Loud Silence

Comments travel across the parking lot at lightning speed.
"Father [B], do you get feedback on your preaching?" I asked.
"No," he murmured and shook his head. "I never hear anything."
There is much conversation. There is little interaction.
There is much presumption about what the "other" is thinking.
There is almost no research.
We are not talking about preaching, together.
That is the Loud Silence.

The Search for Understanding

Stories abound. Studies do not. As a result, we really don't know how we are doing. I once ate lunch with a woman who had taught voice lessons for forty years. She described the throatiness in the voice of her twenty-eight-year-old ministry intern and how she could so easily have helped him to fix it. "Did you ever tell him?" I asked. "Oh, no," she shook her head, "I couldn't do that."

How much good do we miss if we do not help each other? How much could we learn if pulpit spoke with pew, young conversed with old, different cultures opened up to each other? Jesus prayed that we all be one. Why? Because "as one," we are stronger together than we are alone. We have a lot of growing to do to meet Jesus' goal. The discussion about preaching already occurs in the pews. How do we begin to talk about it as a community—pulpit and pew together?

The conversation about preaching has the characteristics of what the Harvard Negotiation Project calls "a difficult conversation": It is a tough subject to talk about; we tend to avoid it; within it are issues of identity and deep feelings; objectivity is challenging. As in any thorny conversation, whether in a family or a parish, the temptation is to lob a hand grenade of feelings and then run away. That blast of opinion often does not bear positive fruit. Should we leave the topic alone because it is so sensitive? In the short run, will opening the discussion make things worse? In the long run, could a positive interchange about preaching outweigh the initial difficulties of opening this conversation?[7]

When we consider how to fulfill the mission of preaching, often we jump to ask: "What should we *do*? In *Verbum Domini*, Benedict XVI said, "the quality of homilies needs to be improved."[8] What approaches could we implement? What seminary courses should we change? What workshops should we design?" Unfortunately, because of the "Loud Silence," our efforts would continue to be built upon our previously held presumptions. We could waste money and busy people's valuable time. At this point in history, there is much that we do not know. There is also much that we are not talking about.

The Harvard negotiators offer an alternate initial step in a difficult conversation: first create a "learning stance." Before

> At this point in history, there is much that we do not know.
> There is also much that we are not talking about.

we jump into the "action" questions of "What should we *do*?" we inquire, "What do we not know?" and "What do we need to understand?" This paints a broader picture of the current situation. Then the action plans that we create will correspond to the actual needs of those involved.

This book begins that search for understanding. It is only a beginning. Unless we formulate our questions carefully, we will not get the answers we need. So this book asks key questions: Why does Sunday preaching matter and to whom? How can we connect the gospel message with our young people? Why is Catholic preaching such an uphill climb? What are the struggles of clergy-on-the-ground in preaching? What is going on in the listener's head during the Sunday homily? And finally, what can each of us do to help "connection" in preaching become more common?

> The goal of this book is to break open the conversation in Catholic preaching as you would break open the Scriptures—with reverence, with love, with the will for the long-term good of the other.

The U.S. Catholic bishops published a recent preaching statement, *Preaching the Mystery of Faith*. Building upon the teachings of *Sacrosanctum Concilium* and Benedict XVI's *Verbum Domini*, the bishops suggest that the purpose of preaching is to bring people into an encounter with God as an integral element within the overall purpose of the liturgy: "One of the most important teachings of Vatican II in regard to preaching is the insistence that the homily is an integral part of the Eucharist itself (SC 31). As part of the entire liturgical act, the homily is meant to set hearts on fire with praise and thanksgiving. It is to be a feature of the intense and privileged encounter with Jesus Christ that takes place in the liturgy."[9]

To foster an encounter with God is a lofty goal for a seven-minute talk at a Sunday liturgy. Thus this book also asks, "How do we implement the bishops' goal?" and "What are the complexities that surround the homiletic encounter?" At this pivotal point in Catholic preaching, a common effort from both clergy and laity is needed to determine how to bring that encounter about. We have to talk. The desired fruit of the conversation is that preaching itself would become an act of love within a community of caring. Harris says that "the true test of good preaching is the effect it produces in the lives of believers."[10] When our people have encountered God through the Sunday preaching as an interchange of love, this will bear fruit and fire the faithful to glorify the Lord by their lives.

How do we open the conversation so as to help our people toward encounter? The final chapters will focus on how to build a culture of listening: how to give and take feedback; how to measure the impact of preaching; and how to set attainable goals for improvement.

This is a communal effort. Read this book by yourself if you must. Then share it with a clergy study group, a parish discussion group, or an adult faith formation group. Questions are at the end of each chapter to encourage discussion. Use these words as a launch pad. Then begin to talk and listen to each other.

We are not done learning. There is much research still to be done. The doctoral thesis that undergirds this book was only a preliminary study that looked at how to connect with high school youth in Roman Catholic Sunday homilies in the United States.[11] Yet breaking open this conversation involves all age groups and other nations and can be applied to the Protestant and Orthodox preaching worlds as well.[12]

The encounter with God through Sunday preaching: it matters. One boy got over his nightmares. A parish in Ohio was a magnet for folks from the surrounding area. A lad of fifteen learned how to pray. If it can happen in these situations, it can happen for you. The human touch of preaching can make a difference.

This book is a springboard for discussion, yes, but the focused effort is yours. You are the one who cares that the light of the gospel burns brightly in the particular world in which you live. Each parish or congregation is unique in its needs. Whether you are a sender or a receiver of preaching; whether you are Protestant or Catholic or Orthodox; whether you are conservative, middle-of-the-road, or progressive; whether you are young or you are old, I say to you: gather with your people to carefully break open this conversation in your place and in your time. Speak to each other with care, with forgiveness, with reverence. Take the long-term approach of "Here's where we are" and "Here's where we would like to be." As one young priest described it, "This is a culture change. Cultural changes are hard." Be sensitive to feelings and be gentle with identities, but take one small step and get started. Then let me know how it goes. Shall we begin?

Workshop in Your Pocket

- "Connection" is everywhere.
- Preaching can make a difference.
- The situation that surrounds preaching is complex.
- We are not studying it empirically, and we are not talking about it together.
- When there is no conversation, there is only presumption.
- Assumptions can be wrong.
- How much good we miss when we do not help each other.
- The discussion of preaching fits the criteria of a "difficult conversation."
- Let us look at this together.

Preaching and the New Evangelization

Then beginning with Moses and all the prophets, [Jesus] interpreted to them the things about himself in all the scriptures. . . . Then their eyes were opened, and they recognized him; and he vanished from their sight. They said to each other, "Were not our hearts burning within us while he was talking to us on the road, while he was opening the scriptures to us?" (Luke 24:27, 31–32)

The disciples on the road to Emmaus heard a message that resonated within them. Their eyes were opened to recognize Jesus (Luke 24:31). They exclaimed, "Were not our hearts burning within us?" (Luke 24:32). This expression describes an experience—a fiery beating of the heart, a swelling of the lungs, a mental exhilaration, which motivates and drives a person to attend and to learn and to listen and to follow and to join with others who have also experienced it and then to shout out their good news to the whole world. Each generation rediscovers this silent connection of the Holy Spirit; it is the renewed enthusiasm of faith; it is the inner fire that keeps the church going.[1]

The Fire of Faith

How are we doing with that fire? Commitment levels to institutional religions have dropped in the United States, especially among the young.[2] This shift in allegiance has provoked much soul-searching among people of faith. In response to this trend, which first affected Europe, Pope John Paul II described a "new evangelization," an initiative of "new ardor, methods and expression" in getting the gospel message across.[3] His successors have continued to encourage a renewed zeal and enthusiasm for the Good News. Is this "new evangelization" one more program, to be staffed and implemented along with all the other programs? Or is it a change of mindset, a new way of doing business, a recasting of the way we as church see ourselves and our role in the world? In their 2012 document on preaching, *Preaching the Mystery of Faith,* the U.S. Catholic bishops see Sunday preaching as a key piece of that new evangelization: to encounter God is the

> "New methods and expressions" include examining how we preach in order to connect with the people of today.

goal of Sunday preaching within the eucharistic liturgy.[4] "New methods and expressions" include examining how we preach in order to connect with the people of today.

When the Same-Old-Same-Old Is Not Working

The decline in loyalty and commitment to institutional faith is often attributed to secularization, individualism, and materialism. These cultural factors deserve our attention. But outside factors are only one part of the story. No matter the context, whether in a family, a business, or a church, when the "same-old-same-old" is not working, the first instinct is to point a finger at the "other" and hurl the question, "What is *their* problem?"

Like the disciples on the road to Emmaus, for people of faith, an inner motor of jubilation and delight may play in our hearts: do "they" not feel it? From an encounter with God, the intimacy of the gospel may resound with inner purpose and salvific power: why are "they" not sensing it? Both the majesty of Almighty God on a starry night and the tender touch of the Good Shepherd in the Eucharist can warm the ribcage with joy: do "they" not experience that?

To speak credibly to "them," we must turn inward to ask, what are "we" not seeing? What are "we" doing that is not connecting with the world in which we live?

> What are we not seeing?

The Swing of Swings

A parallel comes to us from the world of sports. My Uncle Guy was an avid golfer. At a family reunion in late high school, he took my brothers and my cousins and me to a driving range in Wisconsin. As we piled into the station wagon, though I had never golfed before, I thought, "Ball sports come easily to me. How hard can this be?" I listened intently to my uncle's instructions. I gripped the driver with both of my thumbs pointed downward just as he said. I pulled my elbow back and swung that club as hard as I could. Wham! A hunk of grass flew forty feet in the air. The ball still sat on the tee. "Karla," Uncle Guy chuckled, "You swing like a baseball player." He was right. What was going on in my head? The word "swing" triggered a series of muscle memories from the warm sunshine of a St. Louis baseball diamond from when I was five years old: "pull your elbow back" was ingrained in me by my Dad's lessons on how to choke up on a Louisville Slugger. I knew how to swing. How hard could golf be?

Words stir up mental images from our experience (the word "swing": golf or baseball?). Every discipline has its distinctive vocabulary. Doctors grow concerned when they see elevated alveolar capillary hydrostatic pressure in a patient. Teachers use summative assessments as benchmarks for inquiry-centered higher-order thinking. Web designers evaluate wireframes to see how content, links, and widgets are related to one another. If you are not in "the know" about medicine, education, and web design, you may have skipped over those "meaningless" words even in reading this paragraph. Each field has its own particular language to describe a unique set of experiences. The language of faith is no different.

The Curse of Knowledge

As I spoke to second-year seminarians about my doctoral study on how to connect our preaching with our young people, we played a game. I tapped the rhythm to "Old MacDonald" and asked the young men to name that tune. The song was totally obvious to me. The rhythm of "E-I-E-I-O" played in my head. I tapped the beat out three times. I could "hear" it clearly. Finally, one curly-haired fellow guessed it. Then they paired off and tapped a song for each other. The "tapper" felt really smart—the melody was clearly identifiable to him, but the "receiver" felt really dumb—he couldn't "hear" it at all. What was going on in the first guy's head was not transmitted to the other's brain at all. This disconnection between sender and receiver is what the Heath brothers call "The Curse of Knowledge"—the tune that sounds so clearly inside the sender's head is not playing in the receiver's head.[5]

> The Heath brothers call this disconnection, "The Curse of Knowledge"—the tune that is playing so clearly in the sender's head is not playing at all in the receiver's head.

After my talk, I asked one of the young men, "What was the preaching like for you when you were in high school?" He thought about it, and then he floated his hand over his head to say, "I was clueless." Yet in his own years of theological study, he will learn to exegete a Johannine pericope, grapple with the ontological relationality of the immanent Trinity, and discern that a heteronomy of morality is a denial of human self-determination. The more that he lives and breathes the world and the language of the seminary, the more he will forget what it is like not to know that theology. The tune that will be playing in his theologically-educated head will not be the same

> The more the seminarian lives and breathes the world and the language of the seminary, the more he will forget what it was like *not* to know that theology.

tune that is playing in his listeners' heads when he begins to preach in a parish. His listeners will tune him out if he can't translate what he knows into the words and images that they know.[6]

If we are attuned to its symptoms, we find the "Curse of Knowledge" everywhere—in family interactions, in political debates, and in advertisements. Check it out for yourself. Look around and see how many messages use "insider" language, making them inaccessible to those who are not "in the know." Within the church, this disconnection shows up in evangelization documents, in liturgical preaching, in catechetical programs, and in outreach efforts. Do we only speak to those who see the world in the same way that we do? Are the intellectual arguments, political perspectives, and social expectations of our communications preselected for those of a certain educational level, political ideology, or social vocabulary? If so, the "Curse of Knowledge" tends to keep the insiders in and the outsiders out. When we become self-referential, we cannot see what we cannot see.

As we focus on creating a culture of witnesses who "go out" to say and do in the "new evangelization,"[7] we are also called to build a church culture that listens and self-evaluates and continually strives for both holiness and competence in our ability to communicate the gospel message.

> We are called to build a church culture that listens and self-evaluates and continually strives for both holiness and competence in our ability to communicate the gospel message.

Preaching and the New Evangelization

I asked several focus groups at a national catechetical conference: "How much does the quality of Sunday preaching matter to the 'new evangelization'?" I had described the three target audiences for that initiative, as well as the goals for each: (1) to fuel the fervor of the faithful; (2) to reengage the marginalized and bring back to faith those who have lost it; and (3) to bring the message of salvation to those who do not yet know Jesus Christ.[8]

"For those in that second (marginalized) population, those who tiptoe in and out of our pews, on a scale of 1 to 10, how much difference does the Sunday homily make?" Some suggested a "4" to "7"—the homily does not make that much of a difference: "those people" are not really listening; some are not receptive to challenging messages; people should come for the Eucharist, not for the preaching. One man suggested that those on the margins of faith do not even know that Romans was written by St. Paul, so they do not have the background needed to understand the homily. In other words, "they" are not all that interested in "our song": the tune that plays so clearly in our heads is obviously not playing in theirs.

One young woman offered a different experience at her parish:

> The reason that I say "10" [preaching is of high importance to those on the margins of faith] is that I have witnessed it in my own parish. For years and years and years, we had a very mediocre homilist, a status-quo-kind-of-priest, things just went right along. Now with this pastor that we have, I've seen him actually draw in the marginalized with his homilies. . . . His homilies become the community topic (in a good way) for the rest of the week; then the people evangelize, using things from his homilies to tell people in their workplaces, in their neighborhoods, friends and family, all the people they meet. They post things on Facebook. They tweet it. It sparks that evangelization and draws those people. . . . I've witnessed it. These people start coming to church if they have been away or turn to the church if they are unaffiliated. I have seen it firsthand.

Inspiring Faithfulness and Loyalty

How often do those transformational experiences happen? On a given weekend, how many folks walk out of church with their hearts burning with evangelical zeal as a result of the Sunday preaching? One of the clearest indications of loyalty is the willingness to recommend something to a friend or family member.

To measure loyalty to the preaching that they hear, I asked the students who attended Mass to respond to, "If I had a video or a written copy of this homily (the one last heard), or a link to it on the web, I would recommend it or give it to a friend." What did I find? There were pockets where the preaching inspired evangelistic ardor. More than 15 percent (15.6 percent) of the high school youth surveyed *would* recommend their Sunday preaching to a friend.[9] These young people were enthusiastic and loyal; they talked about the preaching that they heard, and they referred it to others. Their commitment was strong. Their loyalty was solid.

Just as for Michael who was mentioned in the first chapter, preaching also resonated with Mary, a fifteen-year-old girl from New York. Though she may not have grasped the complexity of suffering, this visual image from a homily connected with her life experience:

> It was odd to think that Jesus, who is supposed to love us, could let us suffer so much sometimes. But after hearing a preacher's homily about how to make gold, you must put it in the fire until it is ready and beautiful, I realized that I shouldn't give up on my faith just because life doesn't go my way.

Like Michael and Mary, other teens are listening and evaluating. As St. Paul said to Timothy, let us not dismiss their experiences because they are young (1 Tim 4:12). These youthful promoters are fired up. Their responses give us hope.

Enflaming the Faithful

How are we doing with the "fire" in the overall population? About one of every eighteen adults in the United States is a Catholic who celebrates Mass every single week.[10] As political pollsters have noticed, that is a sizable bloc of people. How many of these faithful have encountered God at some point in their lives? How many grow in faith regularly through the Sunday liturgy? And what brings them there?

Nine in ten (91 percent) of the adults who attend Mass every week believe that Jesus Christ is truly present in the bread and wine of the Eucharist.[11] (Attendance at Mass closely correlates with belief in church teaching.) Mass can be a time for prayer and reflection,[12] a source of uplift to fuel them

> Of those who regularly attend Mass, one in six (16 percent) are actively involved in other parish activities.

for the week. One woman told me, "When you get beat around all week, you hope for a message that refreshes." Some have a deeply ingrained sense of duty toward Mass as a Sunday obligation. Going to church can be a family tradition which fashions personal identity and carries deep meaning. Some youth come because their parents require them to. Others come to worship God.[13]

Out of this population of eighteen million U.S. Mass-attenders,[14] about one in six (16 percent) are actively involved in activities of faith outside of Mass.[15] For this group, the parish is a location for community and friendship. Every faith community seems to have this inner circle. These people are involved in Bible studies and adult faith formation groups, altar and rosary societies, church cleaning crews, the Knights of Columbus, catechetical programs, prayer groups, the finance council, and so on. This population is more likely to read prayer books, drink of Catholic TV and radio, and buy books about their faith (like this one). Thus an inspiring Sunday homily is most welcome, but it is not their only source of input; other venues also feed their "fire."

If and when a homilist gets feedback about his preaching, this inner circle is most likely to be those who give it to him. They are also the ones who are the least dependent on it for their faith formation. One daily communicant expressed it this way: "I come for the Eucharist. The rest, well," he shrugged, "doesn't matter so much." As a result, if a homilist depends on this select population for feedback, it would skew a homilist's understanding of the homily's importance.

The Grief of the Faithful

Several years ago, I gave the keynote address to the "inner circle" at the annual festival of a nearby parish. I could not see my listeners' body language because the lights on the stage were so bright and the gym was so dark, so I attuned my ears to listen for what Bishop Ken Untener called "the fidget level."[16] There was one period of profound silence. The hush came when I named the unspoken grief in the hearts of the faithful—the sorrow over the loss of those they love to the faith.

> The unspoken grief of the faithful is the loss of those they love to the faith.

I have since grown attentive to the symptoms of that heartache: the anguish of mothers and fathers, grandmothers and grandfathers, sisters, brothers, friends, aunts, uncles. . . . The array of emotions is broad—from grief and anger to bargaining and frustration, denial and depression, pain and guilt, and sometimes acceptance. That faith, which is the foundation of their lives, does not matter to those whom they love.

Imagine the conflicts on Sunday morning in this teen's family: "My parents are . . . religious but I don't care about God and don't believe in an afterlife. As long as you are kind, it does not matter." Within the last few years in the United States, it may not be only those who are marginal in their faith whose children are walking away, as Christian Smith—a sociologist of religion among adolescents—documented in 2002 in the National Study of Youth and Religion.[17] We are now also losing children of the deeply faithful. Many are not coming back. This loss influences almost every person who is active in the church. Priests, bishops, and cardinals have also lost nieces and nephews to the faith. Some parishioners who have remained steadfast throughout the years of clergy abuse and scandals and financial strains have grown disheartened by the inability of the church to speak a compelling word to their estranged loved ones. This longing for effective preaching is an ache. Why? They live with and cherish those who question, those who doubt, and those who do not practice the faith that they love. Many prayers are catapulted to heaven for the loss of loved ones to the faith. And that grief, too, we do not talk about.

So how does the Sunday preaching matter to the evangelization of the "inner circle"? They are ready and willing to hear a word that both comforts and strengthens them. The homily matters in three ways: (1) to deepen their own relationship with God as a source of faith growth; (2) to empower them to model and to speak the message of the gospel to those around them; and (3) to offer an inspiring word to those whom they love in the rare times when they *can* get them to come to Mass.

Present and Accounted For

Five of the six adults who attend Mass weekly are not active in other parish functions. The Sunday liturgy is thus their only point of contact with the parish. If they get outside input, this faith formation is acquired privately, online or via TV or radio. (This is not to equate holiness with activity in a parish, since saintliness is certainly not synonymous with, or the sole property of, the "inner circle.") But for those who have no other source for growth in discipleship, the message from the pulpit may be their only faith formation moment.[18] A catechist from Tennessee echoed this thought about those in her parish: "The Sunday homily is the chief moment when most of your parishioners and visitors are present and therefore it has the greatest impact on the faith life of those who hear." The U.S. bishops' document *Preaching the Mystery of Faith* says similarly: "Jesus Christ must be proclaimed in a new way and with new urgency, and the

> For those regulars who have no other source of growth in discipleship, the message from the pulpit may be their only faith formation moment.

Sunday liturgy remains the basic setting in which most adult Catholics encounter Christ and their Catholic faith."[19]

How are we doing with this "new urgency?" In my study of youth, the highest level of ambivalence arose from this descriptor: "This homily was full of conviction." Almost half (46.3 percent) of the Mass-attenders circled "neither agree nor disagree": ironically, *the kids had no conviction that the homily was full of conviction.*[20]

The inner vitality of a preacher rubs off on his people. If he is worn out or weary or bored or ill-prepared, it shows. One lad picked up on this lethargy: "It just seemed like not only me and the rest of the people at the church were going through the motions but also our priest was." One lay leader described the lackluster homily that he last heard in a similar way: "It was the airline safety speech; everybody knew it was coming, everybody knew what it was going to say and no one wanted to pay attention to it."

When asked if they would recommend the homily that they last heard, 42.5 percent of the youth who attended Mass regularly, said, "I don't know."[21] Their experience of preaching was lukewarm. They had a low level of allegiance to the preaching. They were not evangelistic or passionate about the message they heard. Loyalty was not solid.

What is the role of the homily in the evangelization of those who are faithfully in the pews? Week after week, they attend. Many hunger for richer food. "Feeling the love" of a welcoming community and a warm handshake at the door may help, but it will not bring dedication, commitment, and loyalty. Laypeople seek for competence in preaching. In their words: put together a clear message that speaks to our world; use stories and images that we can relate to; have a compelling delivery; speak in concrete language that is memorable; strengthen content; and shape a homily that stretches us (a little).[22]

To engage this group, homilies need to deliver a compelling message that not only connects but also motivates. When asked if he could say anything to preachers, as his final comment, a twelfth-grade boy pleaded, "More life, more passion. Monotony kills interest." Pope Francis has listened to those in the pew and heard the same: "Our people like to hear the Gospel preached with 'unction,' they like it when the Gospel we preach touches their daily lives, when it runs down like the oil of Aaron to the edges of reality, when it brings light to moments of extreme darkness, to the 'outskirts' where people of faith are most exposed to the onslaught of those who want to tear down their faith. People thank us because they feel that we have prayed over the realities of their everyday lives, their troubles, their joys, their burdens and their hopes."[23]

The quality of the homily shapes those regular attendees who are on the edge of parish life even more than it forms those who are at the center. If they have no other spiritual input, the homily "weighs" heavily. If to encounter God is the goal of Sunday preaching within the eucharistic liturgy, then that homily is like a lifeline. If that lifeline does not hold, they drop.

Thus, Sunday preaching is a "tipping point"—the place where a focused effort for improvement could

> The quality of the homily shapes those regular attendees who are on the edge of parish life even more than it forms those who are at the center.

cascade into an epidemic of growth among the faithful,[24] leading them to a personally "profound experience of God."[25] Then, like the disciples on the road to Emmaus (and the parish mentioned earlier), they will dash off to tell their families, their friends, and their neighbors. Joy, excitement, and fervor are contagious. If we are to renew the church, we can go out to the highways and the byways to bring in the lost and the forsaken, but the first effort must be to fire up those who still sit in our pews.

Present but Not Happy about the Homily

Not all of those who attend Mass regularly are happy about the preaching. At the other end of the spectrum from the 15.6 percent enthusiastic homily promoters were the almost forty-percent (38.1 percent) of youth who regularly attended Mass but said of the homily, "No, I would not recommend" it to anyone.[26]

Some youth had a strong personal faith life but rated the homily that they had just heard poorly in ten descriptors of homiletic excellence.[27] Others rated themselves weak in faith but rated the homily well.

Folks who "would not recommend" may be either "complainers," or they may be "detractors." If a person complains about the preaching, it means that he or she is still invested and could be turned around. Parents and clergy complain about complainers, but at least they are still complaining; customer service researchers say that complainers have the potential to become supporters.[28] Yet even when the listener is spiritually receptive, preaching which does not bear fruit can deeply dishearten. At a focus group, an eighteen-year-old retreat leader was candid about losing her drive to hear the message of the homily:

> The Eucharist (Jesus!) and my faith community is the reason I love the Mass. I generally hate homilies . . . this summer they even became my "nap time" on my mom's shoulder right before I had to go to work (after Mass). I would consider myself deep in my faith, but I want to make the preacher sit down so many times and have someone else talk.

Detractors, on the other hand, have stopped complaining. They may still be sitting in the pews for one reason or another, but they are not happy. Their negative word-of-mouth heavily influences others—they tell stories of unhelpful experiences, and they are not good stories. No matter the age of the recipient, negative memories cement themselves solidly in the mind. Those who work in ministry have heard a variation of this comment: "Remember when Father So-and-so said 'Such-and-such-and-such' to Uncle Henry's godson's niece's friend at her mother's funeral in 1982? And of course none of us have been back to Mass since?

> Negative word-of-mouth heavily influences others.

How could he say that!" That is a detractor. This negative word-of-mouth spreads and is destructive to the reputation of a clergyman, a parish or the church.

Those who do not complain are also more likely to walk away.[29] When young people go to college and are no longer required to be at Mass, they may vote with their feet. One girl voiced her frustration, "When I come to Mass with the intention of learning and becoming closer to God and leave with having neither of those fulfilled, I do not have as strong a desire to go the following weekend."

What is the role of the homily among this dissatisfied group? I searched for the opposite to the word "evangelization" but could not find one. The antonym of the similar word, "to convert," is "to dissuade, to secularize, to persuade against." Preaching can obscure the face of God rather than bring the listener into an encounter. In looking for connection, a sixteen-year-old Asian-American girl found,

> None. I find it frustrating. Shouldn't a man of God be able to connect with us laypeople? Especially us young members. We are

the next generation of Catholic/Christians/etc. If we get disconnected, we won't want to come or listen and eventually separate for good. It saddens me that most people I know turned atheist b/c they were not able to connect.

Mass-attending faith-filled young people watch their peers walk away. That, too, causes them pain.

Tiptoeing In, Tiptoeing Back Out

If one of the primary purposes of evangelization is to fire the hearts of the faithful, then how broadly do we define "the faithful"? Many who do not attend Mass weekly also consider themselves to be among "the faithful."

Of a hundred people who self-identify as Catholics, sixty-eight will darken the doors of a church at least once a year. Those on the farther edges come most often in Lent and at Christmas and Easter. Statistically, those on the periphery are more likely to be young and/or male.[30] This is the "marginal" population which most frequently comes to mind when church documents speak of the "new evangelization."

> Many who do not attend Mass weekly also consider themselves to be among "the faithful."

This tiptoeing in and then tiptoeing back out can frustrate clergy and those in the inner circle, bemoaning, "Why don't they come?" Sometimes that lament is followed by mutterings about mortal sin. Some insiders feel anger and resentment about the Christmas-Easters outsiders. The inner circle and the "outer circle" may not have a lot in common theologically and politically.[31] The tune that is playing in the one head is certainly not playing in the other.

When asked why her family did not attend Mass, a Hispanic girl in New York said, "We are all busy and take church lightly so we think we can skip it. My parents and I enjoy church." Does Sunday preaching matter for those whom we see rarely? Surprisingly, it can be of great help. An African American girl, who listed no particular parish home, described it this way: "I've had a few enlightening moments at a parish I went to. I was at a point where my faith was being challenged and what the priest said made me turn more toward my faith."

Even snippets of liturgy can warm the heart: a young man who was raised a Lutheran attended a Christmas Eve Mass only one time in his

troubled late teens; six years later, he recalled the reverence of that experience and decided to join the church. In my study, I was surprised to see
that those who did not consistently attend Mass marked that the homily
"helped me to commit myself to following Jesus" with a higher percentage than those who attended regularly.

Thus, in researching evangelization, rather than bemoaning nonattendance we can look for bright spots, for touches of grace, for moments
when God is obviously at work. We flip around that question of "Why
don't they come?" and ask
"Why *do* they come?" What
draws them in?

> We flip around that question of "Why
> don't they come?" to ask "Why *do* they
> come?" What draws them in?

Sometimes people tiptoe
back into a church building
when they are in pain or
in a moment of crisis—after the death of a loved one, during a time of
illness or despair, living through family troubles, or at a really low place.
Those who attend Mass a few times a year come mostly for "prayer and
reflection."[32] Does the preaching heal the brokenness in their lives? Does
it raise them up when they have been discouraged; give them hope when
all feels hopeless? Does it meet them where they are and bring them into
the presence of the living God who wants to console them? Might God
be saying to us, "*I* am calling them here; show them my face."

What can the homily do for those who tiptoe in and out of our
pews? Like the experience of the young woman above, a well-crafted
homily can strengthen belief for those on the margins. A single homily
can stick in the memory. A
single homily can connect
so as to help. A single homily can also hurt at a vulnerable moment. Almost as

> It takes at least twelve good memories to
> make up for one memorably bad one.

a mother hen protecting her chicks, a twelfth grader from Indiana urged
caution as she described the power of liturgical preaching: "I would tell
them to consider my age group. Our faiths are fragile right now, and
homilies could either make or break them."

Since negative memories weigh most heavily in the mind, those on the
edge of faith are working out of a very small sample of past experience.
Psychologists say that it takes at least twelve good memories to make up
for one memorably bad one.[33] To bore or to ramble or to offend or to yell
at the folks who come once a year to Christmas Mass simply supports their
belief that people are bored or offended or get yelled at in this building

every Sunday for the whole year, so why in the world would you *ever* want to come here? Those who attend infrequently do not have a heart burning for the Eucharist in the same way as those who are regulars, or they would be there more often.[34] Therefore it is even more important for a homiletical message to relate to their lives. That one experience may be the only sacred input they get all year.

To connect the homily to their lives, we can find needs that are not being met by the secular world: What emptiness does the world leave? How can the gospel message fill those holes?[35] The confirmation homily, for example, should be the very finest that a bishop can give since that moment may be a one-in-a-hundred experience. There is no homiletical effort too great or too loving for Jesus' wandering sheep.

Just about Gone

Tyler is seventeen. He (somewhat) doesn't believe in God, his friends are not strong in their faith, and he doesn't have a church or faith community that helps him to grow. Church? It's not so necessary. Like the other youth in my study, trying to be a good person is the most important value to Tyler. Growing closer to God, putting God first in his life, and praying are at the bottom. He is not hostile; he just doesn't find "churchy stuff" all that convincing or appealing. He says, "I don't really have much faith or a religious life anymore. I feel it would be hypocritical of me to pretend to believe in things that I don't believe in." He still lists himself as Catholic and says, "I don't really attend Mass regularly anymore, but when I was younger, it was nice."

About three of ten of those who call themselves Catholics rarely or never attend Mass.[36] Their identity as Catholics has little to do with their practice. If their family has always been Catholic, when they are admitted to a hospital or they answer a survey, they may check "Catholic" because it is part of how they see

> "I am Catholic, I just don't go to Mass."

themselves. A seventeen-year-old described it this way: "I am Catholic, I just don't go to Mass." They may occasionally attend a baptism, confirmation, funeral, or wedding.

I asked the group of students who were baptized as Catholics but were not attending Mass, "If you do not regularly attend a religious service, describe why not."[37] Eighty-five percent of their open-ended comments were not hostile. Just over 50 percent said: it is boring, it doesn't interest me, or it is a waste of my time. Half of them also said that they were busy, that their family had gotten out of the habit of going, or it was just not a priority.[38] Some found their spiritual fulfillment elsewhere. Nonattendance was not necessarily parallel to noninterest. Spiritual desire can simmer, but needs are not met. Brittany is a tenth-grade girl who likes to go to her Catholic school. Even though she doesn't attend Mass, she is still somewhat connected to God. Why doesn't she go? "I like church," she says. "I would go on Sundays, but since my parents split we don't go anymore."

Circumstances get in the way for others also. Eighteen-year-old "Ryan" says, "We don't go every week like we should because of my dad's illness. When I go, I feel as if someone is listening to me and helps me to grow." Painful experiences in life can also tug people away. Nick says, "My parents lost my little brother when I was six; we have not regularly gone since. They are now divorced."

Most of the responses to the institutional church are not a hardened opposition but more a lackadaisical, "Why should I?" Church attendance does not pass the "Who cares?" test for them.

What is the role of the homily in evangelizing this group who do not participate enough to hear that message? There are three different pathways:

> The preaching of funerals, weddings, and baptisms are prime moments for evangelization.

1. Moments of trauma and times of transition can open spaces for the Holy Spirit to work. The preaching of funerals, weddings, and baptisms are prime moments for evangelization.[39]

2. Some of these folks can be found online. Blogs and discussion groups can provide interaction with those who have no use for church-attendance.

3. Catholic homilies rarely offer insights for parishioners about how to deal with pastoral issues.

Throughout the lectionary readings, Jesus models mercy and healing. He listens and encourages. He embodies superb interpersonal skills. Why is imitating Jesus the Pastoral Good Shepherd so often ignored in unpacking the Sunday Scriptures? Many of those who have distanced themselves from the faith community are not hostile. They have extended family members who could help them to encounter that Good Shepherd. Parents, grandparents, aunts, uncles, children, siblings, and friends often do not know what to say in these moments. Few people ever hear homilies which empower their pastoral counseling skills. Moments of need are moments of opportunity.

"Nones"

More people are now willing to admit to having no religious affiliation. Of the sample population of baptized-Catholic-non-attenders in my study, almost 15 percent of the responses to why they don't go to Mass were negative—they disagreed with church teaching, they had no use for the institutional church, they no longer believed in God, they had embraced another faith, or they had negative experiences of preaching, clergy, or the parish. This group of baptized teens would not show up in a survey of self-identified Catholics because they are not likely to identify as Catholics.[40] The greatest growth in the category of "nones," those who identify themselves as having no religious affiliation, has been among the young—in 2012, a third of adults under the age of thirty had no religious affiliation (32 percent).[41]

What do these people know about the Catholic Church? Where do they get their information if they are never there? They are influenced by past experience. They work out of memory. Negative word-of-mouth of others influences them. Their input comes from the news, internet interactions, secular media, and TV or

> The farther people get from Mass-attendance, the more they form their impressions of the church from sources outside of the church.

movies. The farther people get from Mass-attendance, the more they form their impressions of the church from sources outside the church.

Even more than those who attend marginally, how do we reach the "nones?" Like for those on the margins, when "nones" do hear a homily or attend a Mass at a family event, a sliver of that liturgy deeply imbeds in their memory. As effective preachers know, special occasions are crucial times for fine preaching. Also, the way that Catholic Christians carry themselves, whether at home, school, and work can either confirm or refute the "nones'" mental picture of what it means to be Catholic—a holy example is worth a thousand words.

Documents on evangelization assume that those with no religious affiliation are spiritual seekers looking for a religious home, implying that all we have to do is to extend a hand of welcome and these people would happily come sauntering in to our pews. Statistically that presumption does not hold.[42] They are busy with other things and ascribe to other value systems. The institutional church is barely, if ever, on their radar.

> The institutional church is barely, if ever, on their radar.

Community, friendship, and personal fulfillment come from other sources. Running groups, yoga classes, soccer teams, internet chat rooms, video game teams, book clubs, mothers groups, service opportunities, workplace interactions—many other organizations vie for their time, talent, and attention. Church—who needs it?

How do we talk to this population? Laypeople live and breathe among those who do not believe. They themselves hunger for insights into how to converse: a mother cannot harden her heart to her son; an uncle cannot be dismissive of a niece's unbelief; a friend cannot write off a friend; a grandmother is not indifferent to her granddaughter's agnosticism. So what are we to do?

We believe in a God who is Revealer, patient, and continually at work. The gentle breath of the Holy Spirit keeps whispering. So first we trust in the God who values them who is by nature a Self-communicator. When I give my "Atheists, Agnostics, and 'Nones'" workshop, I find that formation in how to listen is what is most needed. I suggest to the "inner circle" that when a person tells them, "I am an atheist (or an agnostic)," to hold their own emotions in check and adopt a listener stance. Surprisingly, according to the same study that found so many non-institutionally-affiliated people, 14 percent of atheists and 56 percent of agnostics say that they believe in God or a universal spirit.[43] Thus, we can ask the open-ended question about nonbelief, "And what does that mean to you?" We can tease out this question: "What is the image of God to which you object?" The world that we live in is loud. A cacophony of voices vies for attention. Those who are far from faith are hearing other messages than ours. How can the whisper of the Holy Spirit be heard amid so much noise?

Sources of Influence Are Close to Home

With so much information coming at us in this wired age, communication experts tell us that we are learning to self-select those voices that we attend to. The constant bombardment of messages causes us to self-protectively tune out. Have we stopped listening? Some suggest that is the case.[44] The ubiquity of smartphones and ear buds and instant posts to social media sites implicitly sends the message that what is "out there" is more important than what is "right here." Though we call ourselves more "connected," we may be even more alone.[45]

At the same time, sources of influence are coming closer to home. Social impact studies say that we trust human interaction more

> Though we call ourselves more "connected," we may be even more alone.

than any other source. Word of mouth carries more weight than a blog.[46] As technology grows more omnipresent, human touch grows more vital. When asked to describe "connection," the teenagers in my study did not ask for "more Twitter" or "more Facebook." Over and over again, what they said was: relate to my life and let me relate to yours. . . . Help me with my problems. . . . Teach me what I need to know. . . . Challenge me to be a better person. . . . Show me, by your actions and by your words, why I should be here. . . .

The majority of the high school students whom I surveyed were able to identify some adult who had personally inspired them. What were they looking for? They described "connectors" as role models of authenticity and integrity: people who lifted them in their times of trial, adults that they could laugh and have fun with, mentors who shared life and love. Human bonds can have a lifelong impact on a kid struggling to grow up. A sixteen-year-old girl said, "It feels very good when an older person connects with you because at a young age we often feel very confused."

Human bonds can have a lifelong impact on a kid struggling to grow up.

This faith in those who are local and connected opens up an incredible opportunity for the caring and convincing human touch of Sunday preaching. At this point in history, even though a preacher physically walks to a pulpit or a stage; even though the words cannot be edited or tidied up or rewound before they are sent out; even though there is no wireless router, there is no cell tower, and there is no coaxial cable, through that link whom we call the Holy Spirit, a preacher can "connect." The homiletical human bond matters more than ever. Preaching can make a difference. It has the potential to draw us into an encounter with the invisible God through the words and actions of a visible human being.

A retired priest said to me, "I don't have any idea how to reach this new generation. You will have to help us to retool." We can upbraid the culture of relativism, secularism, and individualism, or we can focus on how we ourselves can better connect with renewed passion, revised methods, and refreshed expression. For this, we turn to two sources: (1) the words of Catholic high school students themselves give us insights into how to connect with them; and (2) the finest "Connector" in history, Jesus of Nazareth, the Carpenter's Son, modeled for us how to connect.

3

Not Made to Be Alone

If then there is any encouragement in Christ, any consolation from love, any sharing in the Spirit, any compassion and sympathy, make my joy complete: be of the same mind, having the same love, being in full accord and of one mind. (Phil 2:1–2)

From the stories told in the Gospels, Jesus of Nazareth knew about human life. The Carpenter's Son saw teenagers squander their cash and their youth. He watched fishermen fish. He wept with widows. He told stories about fish and sheep. He talked about pigs and extra tunics. He crafted parables about sand and fig trees and a prodigal son. He took the ordinary "stuff" of the first-century Jewish world to proclaim that the kingdom of God had come. The news was good; the news was powerful; the time of fulfillment was at hand: "Repent, and believe in the good news" (Mark 1:15). The Messenger and his message were magnetic. Little children tried to touch him. Publicans were pulled toward him. Roman soldiers snuck close to see him. The people of Israel encountered a taste of glory in this Master of connection.

How did he do it? Spirit to spirit, heart to heart, life experience to life experience, the traveling prophet put the good news into the words of the people. We don't know what he looked like, but there must have been something compelling about the look in his eyes, the touch in his hands, and the cadence of his voice. Whatever it took to get the message to connect with his "sheep," that seems to be what the Good Shepherd did. Jesus loved and thus he preached.

In our high-tech world, it is this human connection of love which still prevails. In theory, this seems obvious. In day-to-day practice, however, it is courageously hard. To preach as Jesus preached is an act of love in word and deed. It is not a culturally-defined "mushy tolerance" but to love in the gospel sense of "to love your neighbor as yourself"; to love as in Aquinas' definition of "to will the good of the other"; to love as in offering a hand when the path is rocky; to love as in listening in order to understand; to love as in giving without the assurance that there will be a return; and to love as in the audacity to work together for the long term and common good. The words and the deeds of Jesus were inseparable. Our goal is to be like Jesus, to spread the gospel by connecting as he did.

But what is this elusive "connection?" How do we know connection when we see it? And why does it matter? In order to preach as Jesus did, we too have to be observant of ordinary life. We can take notice of where and when human bonds happen. We can discern seasons of unity and moments of disunity. We can listen to the words of youth and adults who share what connection means to them and why it matters.

> In order to preach as Jesus did, we too have to be observant of ordinary life.

Why Connect?

Human beings flourish best in community. We are not made to be alone (Gen 2:18). A sixteen-year-old girl described connectedness as a feeling of solidarity: "When my aunt connects with me, I feel like I'm not alone and that I actually have someone on my side." This mutual support feels "right." A high school boy says, "My parents connect with me well. They listen to me if I have a problem or something and if they have a problem . . . , I listen to them." A seventeen-year-old girl speaks of the richness that human bonds bring to her life: "To me, connection means approachability and the amount of comfort and openness you feel when talking with him/her. To connect means to form a trusting and open relationship with someone where you feel willing to talk to them. . . . The people I have connected with, especially adults, are the people who talk to me as their equal and seem genuinely interested in me and not just what I might have to offer."

At a workshop at a national conference, I asked the participants to write down a time when they felt really connected to someone. After a few moments of quiet scribbling, I asked them to share that experience with one other person. In the discussion that followed, the room was full of laughter and joy as people smiled and told stories and talked. It felt as though we were sharing a good meal together, though we were only communicating about this common experience of connection. Among the Catholic high school students in my study, 97 percent of them were able to describe an adult with whom they connected.[1]

Sources of Connection

Who connects with our youth? Mothers win, hands down: "My mom connects with me. She understands, yet helps me on in life." Dads come next: "My father connects with me mostly. He inspires me to do better and become better." Other family members also make a difference: "I have . . . one special connection with my grandma on my Dad's side. She is very old and she is very religious. She has had a hard life and so have I, but she is closer to God. As I have gotten older, we have formed a deeper relationship . . . and I enjoy our conversations." As a source of impact, the influence of the family still cannot be surpassed.

Teachers and coaches can also connect well: "The math teacher here at [my school] really connects with me. I have had to pay bills and pretty much become an adult since my father passed in 2006. He understands my hardships and poverty and is just here for me. I can relate to him on a lot of things."

Leaders from church were mentioned third most often:

1. "My youth group leader connects very well with me. He is young, funny, and easy to talk to and knows my name. He keeps me coming back to youth group every Sunday because of his energy and youthfulness."

2. "I connect very well with [name, pastoral associate]. She is truly a role model for everyone. She's kind, sweet, and loves to talk to me. I feel really connected to her when we talk about God."

3. A young man maintained a strong connection even though his connector had moved away: "My priest that baptized me, he moved churches, but I'm still in touch with him. He helps me with many of my decisions these days, because he'll lead me in the right path!"

Who Connects with Our Youth?

Moms

Dads

Family Members

Teachers

Coaches

Youth group leaders

Parish staff

Clergy

Others

"Connector" seems to be a role that almost anyone can do if he or she is willing to invest the time to do it.

Mentors, neighbors, friends' parents, a choir director, school alumni, and close older friends were also mentioned as those with whom young people connect. "Connector" appears to be a position that almost anyone can do if he or she is willing to invest the time and energy to fill that role.

Pathways to Connection

How do connectors go about connecting? The most common response was: "They 'relate to me.'" This was variously described as: "being chill," "in sync," "they come down to my level," and "they relate to my life." A sixteen-year-old girl said, "Connection to me means being able to relate to a person, to have in depth conversations, and to be on a personal level." A seventeen-year-old boy said, "When a teacher, priest or whoever, connects with me, it means that he/she relates to my life. If they can teach about things . . . [and then] can legitimately connect what they are teaching to my life, they will have my full, undivided attention." A tenth-grade boy from California says, "This teacher is really COOL. He is just so in sync with what goes on at school. He just knows how to relate and is a really cool guy." Young people appreciate when adults respect their intelligence and articulately engage them—have meaningful conversations, be interesting, talk about things that matter: "They just talk on our level; they act like they are interested in what we say. They are easy to talk to."

To connect means to be in sync.
(For the uninitiated, "Sup" means "what's up?" and a bumping of fists is a sign of solidarity.)

The second most common path of "how to connect" centered on a mutuality of understanding, especially through empathy: "to know me," to "hear me," to "get me." To be in sympathy and show respect and care for the young person matters greatly: "They understand me. They get where I'm coming from." "I have a mother of one of my closest friends who knows everything about me. . . . She'll have long talks de-stressing me or give me hugs and kisses when I just need them the most. She constantly betters me and keeps me on a positive track."

In addition to empathy, a similarity of interests, experiences, and/or goals was another theme of the "mutual understanding" pathway. Many spoke of doing something together as a common ground for building camaraderie—the "same sense of humor," "interests in common," "similar likes and dislikes," "common enjoyable experiences." "It feels good to talk to a person [my uncle] who feels the same way you do about a lot of things. He likes the same things I do and we act kind of the same."

To connect means to share common interests.

Along with empathy and similarity of interests, the "mutual understanding" pathway included relational openness: "Share personal life," "let me relate to your life," "treated you like family, like a brother," and "he made it a one-on-one thing" revealed a satisfying experience of a reciprocal interchange that was trusting and true and *jointly* uplifting. The connector was willing, not just to listen and take in the concerns of others, but also could openly communicate his or her own limits in an effort to connect life experiences. An authority figure connected best when he or she had a touch of vulnerability in a situation where there was no single clear or obvious answer.[2] Greater influence is granted to an adult by coming "down to the level" of a young person, asking their opinion, being "real," and (occasionally) admitting weakness. Rather than being a form of "selling-out," this is seen as strength: "A personal story makes for a good connection; one that you can feel what the person went through. It's like you were on that journey as well."

After relationality and mutual understanding, the third pathway of "how to connect" was pastoral. The connector helps: "Take the time to help me" and "Be there for you when you are down" and "Knows what to say to lift me up." In times of trouble, the connector has come to his or her aid and thus has formed a bond. "It's when a person knows about your life and doesn't judge you but tries to help you when you ask for it. It's a person you trust."[3]

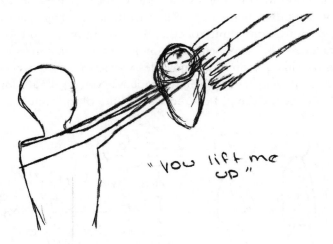

To connect is pastoral: help me up when I am down.

These pathways to connection do not simply pertain to adult-youth relationships. When I offered an expanded version of "how to connect" at a national convention, I asked for participants' enduring understandings from the talk. Though I had assumed that I was speaking about how to relate to kids, one woman raised her hand and said, "I am going to go home and try these things on my husband!"[4] These pathways of connection hold as true for adults as they do for kids.

To discern when we are connecting, an astute observer of life sees differently, looking not at people and objects but at the spaces between them. This is a Gestalt shift which perceives relationships. In the story of the woman caught in adultery, Jesus discerned the connection between the adulteress and the male accusers and thus effectively responded to the core of the relationship (John 8:3-11). This scrutiny of relationships is similar to an artist looking at white space; a football offensive lineman looking for gaps in the defensive line; a musician listening for the rest in a line of notes;

or a soccer player taking the ball to space. If we have eyes to see, from the thousands of words of youth, there are consistent symptoms of connection.

Symptoms of Connection

What are these symptoms? Most frequently cited was the element of trust, described as the openness to "be yourself" in the presence of the other and the safety to just "be." Whether in a time of difficulty or a moment of joy, over and over again, the students spoke of being comfortable: "When I connect with [X], everything just flows. We can continue on the conversation, and it's not uncomfortable at all." There was an ease in the presence of the other: "I can feel a person truly cares when they connect with me. Signs of feeling safe." and "No talk, just hang out."

A second symptom was a natural flow of conversation: "Good connection comes from a bond you two share. They are easy to talk to, funny, and they are there for you when needed. That person tends to always know what to say when things are hard." Accompanying that comfortable and easy flow of conversations were the symptoms of smiling, humor, feeling good, fun, and laughter: "There are adults that connect with me. What happens is we laugh; there isn't a serious nature in the conversation. There are jokes and the conversation is about interesting topics."

Although in other cultures avoiding eye contact is often a sign of respect, in American mainstream culture eye contact and touch usually demonstrate connection: "The person I can think of that connects with me is a teacher. She makes eye contact, listens well, and gives great advice I can relate to." A small number of students wrote of physical contact as expressive

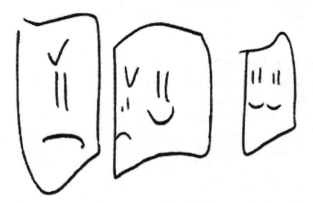

I'm Mad + She's there = I feel better

Symptoms of Connection

Comfort

Safety in being oneself

Naturally flowing conversation

Laughter

Eye contact:

"Everything flows"

---

of connection: "One of my teachers is a good friend and person to talk to. If anything is wrong, she asks me are you ok and touches my shoulder to show that she is there as support." (Although young people themselves described it as a symptom of connection, adults who work professionally with teens are cautioned to be particularly careful about physical touch. There is much ongoing debate on this topic.)

Sharing feelings was also a sign of a bond: "Whenever my mom is around, I always get a positive feeling. When I'm sad, she hugs me and tells me everything will be alright. I know if anything happens, I can go to her. I can share my feelings with her."

To summarize, the "how" of connection centers on relating, understanding, and helping. The "who" of connection can be anybody willing to invest the time to listen and be there for the other. One who is "real," "listens to me," "believable," "true," and "knows how kids think" is respected and revered. Character traits of "fun" and "humorous," "friendly" and "easygoing" and "approachable" combine with "respect" and "compassionate" and "kind" to identify their favorite connectors.

In brief, to the respondents in this study, the overall indicator of connection is a sense of lightness, of joy, of love—everything "flows." Comfort, safety in being oneself, naturally flowing conversation, laughter, eye contact, and physical interaction—these demonstrate that connection is happening.

Symptoms of Disconnection

There are also relationships for which you can identify symptoms of a connection that is blocked or broken. Think back to your own most difficult interpersonal circumstance. It could be a family reunion gone wrong. It could be your worst workplace experience. It could be temporary as in a dull staff meeting or a seminar that just goes on and on and on. It could be a prolonged condition—a situation of abuse or violence or a toxic relationship. What does *that* feel like?

In the aforementioned workshop, after the participants had burbled about moments of good connection, I asked them to write down memories of disconnection and the symptoms that they experienced in those times. (If you ever want to pop the balloon of joy in a room, assign that question.) They soberly wrote about those experiences. When they shared them with one other person, the room felt as somber as the receiving line at a funeral home. Nouns such as "boss" and "teenage son" and "mother-in-law" and "middle-school" and "coworker" floated into the air accompanied by verbs such as "betrayed" and "bullied" and "gossiped" and "hurt" and "messed with." These were the same people, still sitting in the same locations, but the room felt like somebody's favorite dog had just died or the temperature had dropped thirty degrees.

The overarching symptoms of division are the opposite of "lightness": disunity and discord create dreariness and disquiet. Sleepiness, dullness, and heaviness take over when the disengagement comes from boredom. Tension and fear arise in a situation of dread. Rage and anger and hurt produce suspicion and distrust. Awkwardness, an unwillingness to interact, and the avoidance of conflict are the opposite of the honest flow of conversation—instead of opening up, people self-protectively shrink inward. Rather than the deep satisfaction of connection, when folks are not united, they experience fear, frustration, and dissatisfaction. There is no comfort. There is no openness. There is no "flow."

Symptoms of Disconnection

Dreariness and disquiet

Sleepiness, dullness, and heaviness

Tension and discomfort

Rage, anger, and hurt

Suspicion and distrust

Awkwardness

Avoidance of conflict and
   self-protectiveness

Fear, frustration, and dissatisfaction

Feeling blocked; there is no "flow."

Connecting the People of God

Why does it matter that we learn to discern connection? "Searching for connection" is not just a psychological gimmick. Jesus prayed that we all be one. Saint Paul continually fought against divisions among his groups of converts. He was never satisfied with their lack of solidarity.[5] He asked the Philippians to "make my joy complete: be of the same mind, having the same love, being in full accord and of one mind" (Phil 2:2). The infighting of the church has historically been a visible sign of our weakness.

> The disunity of the church is all the more painful because we expect better. To attend to the signs and symptoms of connection is to discern the movement of God among us.

Through the ages, we have blocked the Spirit and hurt each other. In the epiclesis of the Eucharistic Prayer II, we pray "that, partaking of the Body and Blood of Christ, we may be gathered into one by the Holy Spirit." The disunity of the church is all the more painful because we expect better. Christian life, both personal and communal, should move from division toward concord as a visible sign of the unity of the Trinity.[6] Thus to attend to the signs and symptoms of connection is to discern the movement of God among us.

The fruits of the Spirit—love, generosity, joy, gentleness, peace, faithfulness, patience, modesty, kindness, self-control, goodness, and chastity—are often described as personal qualities of holy individuals. Yet for the first-century mindset, the modern psychological *attributes* of "*I* am loving, faithful, patient, etc." was not in their mental framework. Saint Paul, and the Galatians to whom he wrote about the fruits of the Spirit, were group-oriented (Gal 5:22-23).[7] Thus the fruits of the Spirit, as first described, were relational and dynamic *behaviors*: love, kindness, and faithfulness were not character traits but actions on behalf of the other. The Holy Spirit is the invisible Connector, the Tie who binds us.

The gospel stories about Jesus' way of relating—his kindness, his gentleness, his love, his faithfulness—model for us the interrelational fruits of the Spirit. Each of them involves a way of connecting. This requires a Gestalt shift in our eyesight to see what is happening in the spaces between us. The vision of bringing together God's people means to be attentive to the ways and means of connection.

Connecting the Gospel Message

There is a second sense to the vision of connecting "pulpit and pew." It was the final week of the summer at Notre Dame when I packed six graduate credits of Rahner and the Doctrine of God/Trinity into a three-week term. As I ate my meatball sub in the booth at LaFortune Student Center, my mind raced with lofty thoughts of the potentiality for hypostatic union and how that intersected with manifestations of the economic Trinity in the revelation of the Christian faith.

Three bricklayers slid into the booth behind me and began to talk about getting their kids to soccer practice, the golden retriever getting loose and dashing through the neighborhood, and the smell of the visiting mother-in-law's cinnamon rolls with coffee at breakfast. I began to long for my garden back in Ohio, just to pull some weeds and get my hands into that black dirt. The theoretical side of my brain was aglow with theological exercise; the practical side of my head felt like it was starting to atrophy from lack of use. My muddled mind merged the two: what can the smell of cinnamon rolls tell us about the economic Trinity? What does radical dependence on God have to say about muddy boots covered with mortar? In that moment, though a lifelong native of the pew, I marveled at so much wisdom and so much life: (1) the enormity of the treasures of the church; and (2) the enormity of the task to translate that wealth into the treasure that is ordinary practice.

Generation after generation, the church has struggled to put the message of the gospel into the words of everyday life. As he opened the Second Vatican Council, John XXIII asked the church to "[never depart] from the sacred patrimony of truth received by the Fathers. But at the same time . . . [to] look to the present, to the new conditions and new forms of life introduced into the modern world, which have opened new avenues to the Catholic apostolate."[8] Conciliar documents called for the church to engage the modern world. The Sunday homily has been on the front lines of that engagement.[9] How are we to connect theology to life? That is the task of preaching.

The Source and Summit

In the search for connection between pulpit and pew, we have looked at two senses of that connection—the human-to-human bond and the bonding of the gospel with everyday life. Where do these two types of connection come together? What is the common vehicle for connecting the gospel message to the people and connecting the people to each other? Historically, the Sunday liturgy has been the place where Christians have gathered. In the early centuries of Christian faith, "bishops did not ask their faithful to 'go to Mass' on Sunday . . . but to 'go to church,' an expression that designates the assembly"; even more particularly, to go to the local church, since "every eucharistic assembly truly realizes the church of God."[10] The revelation of God is to be found in the concrete interaction of the community in which Christians live.

Sacrosanctum Concilium states that the liturgy of the Word and the liturgy of the Eucharist are one: "The two parts which, in a certain sense, go to make up the Mass, namely, the liturgy of the word and the eucharistic liturgy, are so closely connected with each other that they form but one single act of worship."[11] The purpose of the homily then is "a preaching event that is integral to liturgy that . . . calls and empowers the hearers to faith, a deeper participation in the Eucharist, and daily discipleship to Christ lived out in the church."[12]

> "I usually look around at other parishioners and feel a strong sense of faith and community after a good homily."

Within the liturgy of the assembly, the homily has a place of distinction: "We also recognize that for the vast majority of Catholics the Sunday homily is the normal and frequently the formal way in which they hear the Word of God proclaimed. For these Catholics the Sunday homily may well be the most decisive factor in determining the depth of their faith and strengthening the level of their commitment to the church."[13]

The words and the deeds of Jesus were inseparable. Similarly, our words and our deeds as a community are also to be inseparable. The Sunday homily itself plays a vital part in this as a mediator or connector. Pope Francis describes this synthesis in *Evangelii Gaudium*: "The preacher has the wonderful but difficult task of joining loving hearts, the hearts of the Lord and his people. The dialogue between God and his people further strengthens the covenant between them and consolidates the bond of charity" (143). One young man described this unity of message and community in this way: "I usually look around at other parishioners and feel a strong sense of faith and community after a good homily." The homily at the Sunday liturgy is to be a communal encounter that leads "the church" to God. That is the vision.

To create one homily is hard work. To craft a fresh and insightful message day after day after day is challenging: that is the practice.

As we move from the vision toward its implementation, we first look at the current situation that surrounds our preaching. Why has Catholic preaching historically been such an uphill climb? What are the joys and concerns of clergy in preaching? What is going on inside the listener's head as the preacher preaches? And what do young people have to say about connecting with them in preaching? These questions lead us to the next section, where we will unpack the complexity of the homiletic encounter, one piece at a time.

PART TWO

Unpacking the Complexities of the Homiletic Encounter

If a homily were a living being, I would feel sorry for the poor little guy. In the particular town where he lives, on a certain street, within a specific church building, at one Sunday Mass, after a designated Gospel, he's just a bunch of words strung together for about seven to ten minutes. Yet the pressures on the poor fellow are tremendous. He lives within the eucharistic liturgy, which is the source and summit of Catholic life. His purpose is to bring people into an encounter with Jesus Christ. He is expected to: unpack the Scriptures to relate to the lives of the hearers; evangelize folks from all walks of life and persuasions; consistently manifest and be faithful to a two-thousand-year tradition; catechize those who have no other source of spiritual input; come to a stirring conclusion that will stick in the minds and hearts of his assembly; and then shut up and sit down. If a homily were a living creature, he might feel like an ant that was serenely scurrying down a blade of grass when a truckload of bricks got dumped on his head.

The world surrounding the homily is heavy. When a husband comes home from Mass, his wife asks, "How was Mass?" which means, "How was the homily?" Many folks base their opinion of a parish and the institutional church on the quality of the homily. For parish-shoppers and those who tiptoe in and out of liturgy, that seven-to-ten-minute message is a fundamental factor in their decision for and against attendance.

A catechetical leader can work with parents in sacramental prep, train catechists to be effective teachers, and foster attendance at youth group. Those efforts can be strengthened or undermined by that little homily coming from the pulpit on a Sunday morning.

An overworked pastor can dedicate his morning to the family of a dying man, his afternoon to interviewing teachers with the school administrator, and his evening hours to pouring over money issues with the finance council, yet the sum of his ministry is evaluated by that short talk at Mass.

The little fella dwells in a weighty world. From under the bricks, you can hear a whimper arise from the heap: "That is *so* unfair!"

The world around the homily is complex. Might he sense that he is getting squashed beneath the load of bricks? Could we carefully and lovingly start to unpack each of these weights? One at a time, could we set the little guy free?

Those one or two thousand words of the homiletical message do not float out into a vacuum. They are molded by history. They are conditioned by the preacher's life. They are affected by the listeners' lives. They are influenced by the relationship between pulpit and pew. The ability to connect in preaching arises from structural, cultural, and formational causes in each of these areas. Thus, in order to strengthen that one particular homily in that one particular parish (hopefully, yours), first we pick up each piece to see how it shapes the homiletic encounter with God. That is the task before us in this next section.

4

Surrounded by the Greats of History

Therefore, since we are surrounded by so great a cloud of witnesses, let us also lay aside every weight and the sin that clings so closely, and let us run with perseverance the race that is set before us, looking to Jesus, the pioneer and perfecter of our faith. (Heb 12:1-2a)

History is not dead. Catholics believe in the communion of saints. You and I are running the Christian race on the track of today. The holy men and women, who came before us, continuously encircle us: they whoop and holler and cheer and root for us from the bleachers of heaven. Thus, the homily on a Sunday morning is not an isolated event that stands all by itself. We are surrounded by a rich preaching tradition. The homiletic influences of our predecessors float about our heads. We ask the saints to join us in praying for the preaching of the church.

First, the good news: preaching has always been at the heart of Christianity. The challenge: its influence has ebbed and flowed. In the past twenty centuries, some homilies and sermons have soared. They have resonated in peoples' hearts, inspired them to give their lives to God, and changed culture. Others have plodded in the mud. We have had eras flush

> Ours is a word-filled tradition. Preaching has always mattered.

with preaching and long periods of near silence. Preaching has changed in style and purpose according to the needs of the faithful. Prominent voices have altered the homily's direction at key moments. Where preaching happened and who was allowed to preach has varied. One thing has remained: the Christian faith has consistently valued the verbal proclamation of the

Good News. It is central to our faith. Though St. Francis has often been (perhaps mis-) quoted about using words only when necessary, ours is a word-filled tradition. Preaching has always mattered.

The Mandate to Preach

How did this come to be? Jesus of Nazareth was born into a religion which told faith stories of a conversational Divine Being. El Shaddai, the All-Sufficient One, spoke to a seventy-five-year-old man to send him to a Promised Land and to give him descendants as numerous as the stars (Gen 12, 17). Yahweh, the God-Who-Is, spoke through a burning bush to call a man to rescue his people from slavery. Prophets were commissioned to speak on the Almighty's behalf: Isaiah received a burning coal on his tongue to purify him to speak for the Holy One (Isa 6:1-8). Ezekiel ate of the scroll and was lifted by the Spirit to go prophesy to the exiles (Ezek 3:1-5). When Jeremiah tried not to speak of God, fire burned in his bones and he could not hold the message in (Jer 20:9). Interaction between the human and the divine was at the core of Jewish belief: God called. God delivered. God cried. God pleaded. God wept. God acted. God spoke. How could it be otherwise?

In the Jewish synagogues of Jesus' day, worship services were composed of Scripture readings, a homily, hymns, and prayers.[1] The early church continued in this liturgical tradition. We have no transcriptions of the earliest Christian homilies. From later descriptions, the first preachers were witnesses: the apostles and their followers spoke of what they had seen and heard (1 John 1:3). Only St. Paul's letters remain; in them, he described his vocation as a preacher to the Gentiles (Gal 2:2; Acts 22:21; Rom 11:13; Rom 15:15-16). The sacred mandate at the end of Matthew, "Go out to all the nations" (Matt 28:18-20), built upon this theological certitude: God has acted in history. God has spoken through Jesus Christ. The church *must* preach the Good News. How could it do otherwise?

The "How" of Christian Preaching

As Christianity spread, it moved into a world where the skills of public speaking were highly valued. While Christians picked up the mandate to preach from their Jewish roots, they picked up their methods for preaching from the Greco-Roman educational system. In a "grammar" secondary education, a student in the Greco-Roman tradition first learned to read a text aloud; second, he figured out the meanings of the words; and third, he explained the text verse by verse (called exegesis). From this analysis, he gained a moral education about what was expected of him as a model citizen: the teacher would highlight the ethical example of the reading, pointing out how to be a "good citizen." Since the actions of the Greek and Roman gods did not always set a stellar example, teachers often derived moral lessons from them allegorically. Thus verse-by-verse exegesis and allegorical interpretation were first a Greco-Roman educational practice.

> While Christians picked up the mandate to preach from their Jewish roots, they picked up their methods for preaching from the Greco-Roman educational system.

Origen of Alexandria (d. AD 254) is credited with developing the classical form of Christian preaching.[2] Origen himself was educated to the secondary level. When he transferred his skills to preaching, he followed the grammarian's careful task of explicating a text; he gave a verse-by-verse explanation of a Lectionary reading, followed by moral lessons on how to live it. That was what he knew, so that was what he did when he walked through the Scriptures.[3] His exegetical method patterned the predominant style for the Christian homily for the next thousand years.[4]

If a student were wealthier, he could afford to continue his education, moving from a grammar education to schooling in rhetoric. This higher track trained him in the eloquence needed to be a politician or a lawyer.

Once Christianity became the official religion of the Roman state in AD 313, bishops increasingly came from the rhetorically-educated elite. We have records of great variety from this time period. Bishops offered sermons on liturgical occasions. They preached eulogies at state funerals. They drew on catechetical preaching to educate the (many) adults who had not yet been baptized. The bishops taught doctrine to refute heresies. They expounded with flourish and ornamentation. The preaching of a bishop was a major event for his people. His purpose was to build his flock, both morally and spiritually.

Among the most influential of the early fourth-century bishop-preachers were the wealthy and educated Cappadocian fathers: Gregory and his brother Basil of Nyssa and Gregory of Nazianzus. What made them so effective? Gregory of Nyssa was said to be a careful observer of life and a profoundly spiritual man: he knew how his people lived and felt; he carefully observed the people he passed in the streets of his town. He sought to lead his people to deep holiness.

John Chrysostom was the pinnacle of eloquence in the mid-fourth century; his contemporaries called him the greatest orator in history. How did he connect? He used images from the athletic and military, maritime and agricultural worlds. He was direct and personal in style. He also trained hard: "For though the preacher may have great ability (and this one would only find in a few), not even in this case is he released from perpetual toil. For since preaching does not come by nature, but by study, suppose a man to reach a high standard of it, this will then forsake him if he does not cultivate his power by constant application and exercise."[5]

In the fifth century, Augustine declared that Christianity was primarily passed on by preaching. Before his conversion, he was a teacher of rhetoric; he later wrote the first textbook on how to preach, *De Doctrina Christiana*, believing that it was a skill that could (and should) be learned and practiced. In his own preaching, he connected through simple and straightforward language. He was said to make difficult points clear through analogies of everyday life. God's grace was an interior experience of delight to him, so with puns and rhymes and well-turned phrases, he exuded joy; his people, in turn, found him a delight to listen to. Where did the power in his preaching come from? Without using a manuscript, he listened sensitively to the feedback that his audience gave him: if they seemed to grasp his thought, he moved deeper; if they appeared confused, he added an illustration or an example to help them to understand. Some said that as he was speaking, he seemed to sweep the people up into his person and his message. His grasp of doctrine and Scripture was vast. "His real secret, which he shares with all orators who really succeed in fascinating us, is that he had such an enormous amount to say."[6] Yet as Augustine lay dying (d. AD 430), his city of Hippo was being sacked by Vandals. The Roman Empire was coming to an end. The era of homiletical flourishing was also coming to an end.

From the Jewish tradition, the Christian church had internalized the imperative to preach. From the Greco-Roman world, Christian preachers had learned exegesis, allegory, and rhetoric. Yet as the Roman Empire collapsed, so too, did education. Thus for preaching to connect with the needs of the people, it too had to change.

Instructing the Newly Baptized

Christianity spread into the far reaches of Europe in the early Middle Ages. We do not have evidence of the day-to-day preaching that spurred that growth. It is likely that the messages were simple catechetical instructions, given in the local languages.[7] In the sixth and seventh centuries,

Germanic tribes mixed with Latin culture to form a new European mix. Clergy themselves were barely educated. There were no seminaries or universities—the training of a priest followed an apprenticeship model of copying another—he memorized the words of the Mass from another priest. Monasteries kept academic learning alive.

As Charlemagne doubled the territory of the Franks, conversion was one of his conditions for peace, thus his "Christendom" had to deal with a large freshly-baptized population. This leader of the Franks started a reform in which priests were taught to read and write so that they could conduct worship services and educate the people. Sermons had come to be expected from the bishop at the cathedral. But in 813 at the Council of Arles, preaching was also encouraged in parish churches.

There was little education. There were few books. Bibles were rare. So what resources were used for preaching? The homilies of Augustine, Basil, Chrysostom, the Gregories, Leo, and other church fathers were copied by hand, collected, and arranged into sermon collections called "homiliaries." Paul Warnefrid of Lombardy (d. 800), also known as "Paul the Deacon," gathered 244 sermons into a collection which was used for the next thousand years.[8] A bishop or priest (if he was literate) could mine from these homiliaries to read a sermon aloud during the liturgy or use them for spiritual reading. Basic Christian instruction emphasized moral training to answer the eschatological question: "Do you choose heaven or do you choose hell?" The creativity of preaching which had flourished in the late Greco-Roman world shrank into imitation.

We have little record of new and creative preaching until the eleventh century, when a renaissance of preaching began to bubble amid a broader intellectual awakening. Bernard of Clairvaux (b. 1090) restored monastic life and wrote and preached spiritual reform to his monks. Alan of Lille (d. 1202) produced one of the early preaching manuals. Spirituality was in the air—Hildegard of Bingen and other women mystics began to speak of the direct experience of God. The renewal of preaching began to simmer and then burbled into a boil in the thirteenth and fourteenth centuries. Something new was about to begin.

The Mendicants Introduce Thematic Preaching

As Europe grew more prosperous in the twelfth and thirteenth centuries, cities grew as trade centers. The church was not prepared for this: its monastic system had been tied to the land under feudalism. This time of growth unearthed new needs: there was growing restlessness with the wealth and power of the church; newly formed universities encouraged broadened thought; movements of lay preachers, the Waldenses and the Cathars, fomented dissent and threatened to carry whole regions of Catholicism over to their cause. The church needed effective preachers to respond to the ferment. Who could minister to these new urban masses?

Into this gap came two mendicant preachers: Francis and Dominic. Their monks were not tied to a particular physical location, but free to wander according to the needs of the people. Dominic's Order of Preachers saw themselves as a group committed to the mission of preaching. The Franciscans saw themselves as imitators of Christ; preaching was an element of that imitation. Francis insisted on a simple life. Dominic insisted that his monks be trained to preach, which paralleled the rise of the universities.

The rise of the intellect was a heady time. The catechetical sermons must have fulfilled their earlier task, for the mendicants introduced a new type of preaching that built off an expected foundation of basic instruction. They began with a theme, usually from the Bible. From their main point, they fanned out into sub-points with quotations and illustrations from nature and everyday life. Like the concurrent movement of scholasticism, the thematic preachers had a passion for subdividing and analyzing which combined with an exhilaration about the abilities of the God-given human mind.

Books on preaching flourished. Reference books arose. The Bible was divided into chapters. Preaching aids with quotations, popular tales, fables, saints' lives, and collections of model sermons became common. A wandering brother could pull one of these pocket-sized books from his robe and create a thematic sermon on the spot as soon as he came to a town.

This explosion of preaching transformed the High Middle Ages. Stories of successful preachers from this era still abound—Anthony of Padua, Brother Juniper, and of course Dominic and Francis themselves. The preaching of the gospel grew from rare to frequent, from the sole domain of bishops in cathedrals to black- and brown-robed men on city streets.

Discontent and Dissolution

What happened? This booming renaissance of thought and enthusiasm and population and prosperity came to a screeching halt. The fourteenth and fifteenth centuries were a cultural disaster. The citizens of Europe were beset by famine after famine and war after war (the Hundred Years War was 1337–1453). The Black Death and other epidemics reduced the already hungry and weakened population by about two-thirds; in Florence, for example, life expectancy was cut in half. In 1300, a man could expect to live for forty years. By mid-century, his expected life span was cut to twenty years old.[9] As a result of this desperation, society grew a violent edge: children were abandoned; cannibalism was reported; rape and murder were frequent in a world devoid of food.

Moral crises in the papacy weakened the church's authority. The rise of nationalism competed for power with Rome. Calls for reform fell on deaf ears. Discontent was in the air.

What did this do for preaching? There are few records from this era. But by the end of this desperate time, St. Francis' image of baby Jesus in the crèche had been wholly replaced in liturgy, art, and architecture by the power of God the Awesome, the Mighty, the Rule-Giver. Liturgy was frequent and ceremonious, but God was distant: "but the liturgy itself was a clerical liturgy . . . a broad gulf separated clergy and laity."[10] The laity were spectators in a soaring Gothic church. With God so inaccessible, the saints and Mary were the "folks to talk to" and devotion to them was at an all-time high.

The sermon gave some instruction and a few remarks about the meaning of the current feasts or the lives of the saints, but the renewal which had been the mendicants' aim was hollowed by "a dissolution at the heart of ecclesiastical and liturgical life."[11] This disconnect within the church began to enter into its preaching, and thus preaching itself began to depart from the church.

Preaching Is Yours; Sacraments Are Ours

An infant girl baptized in a soaring cathedral in 1500 was received into a church which believed in preaching. By the time that baby's granddaughter received the sacrament of extreme unction at her death, that little string of liturgical words at the Sunday Mass had fallen through the cracks to become both optional and nonessential. What happened?

At the start of the Reformation (1517), preaching mattered to all Christians. As the battle lines between Catholics and Protestants hardened, Martin Luther's call for "*sola scriptura!*" (Scripture only) became the Reformers' rallying cry; since the Catholic Church was corrupt and thus could not speak for God, Tradition was discredited. The "Good Book" became the ultimate source of authority.

A cultural shift was occurring, accompanied by the broad use of the printing press. People became more literate. Thus began an era of thought where the source of authority became the printed word—an attitude of "if it is written, it is true." Pamphlets were novel and the Reformers utilized them abundantly.[12] The Bible was translated from Latin into the languages of the people. A large part of the popularity of the Reformers came from their preaching.[13] By the middle of the sixteenth century, half of Europe had been lost to the Catholic Church.[14]

How did the Catholic Church respond? It was almost thirty years from Luther's initial posting of his ninety-five theses in 1517 to the opening of the Council of Trent in 1545. Some scholars say that it was "too little, too late."[15] What did the Council of Trent have to say about preaching? "The holy Synod has resolved and decreed, that all bishops, archbishops, primates, and all other prelates of the churches be bound personally . . . to preach the holy Gospel of Jesus Christ."[16] This was backed up by a demand for "rigorous punishment" for failing to preach. The obligation to preach as the primary duty of bishops was sent forth both in 1546 and 1563.

One of the historical bright spots in Catholic preaching was the renewal sparked by St. Ignatius of Loyola. The preaching vigor of the Jesuits won back large sections of Germany and central Europe in the latter years of the sixteenth and seventeenth centuries. Second, the century after the Council of Trent was a period of expansion into missionary territory. The Catholics embraced missions at a much greater rate than their Protestant counterparts in travels to India and China and the New World. What was lost in Europe was gained elsewhere.

The Return of Rhetoric

The humanists of the sixteenth century had recaptured the study of classical rhetoric. Erasmus wrote a textbook on preaching in 1535, *Ecclesiastes*, stating, "If elephants can be trained to dance, lions to play, and leopards to hunt, surely preachers can be taught to preach." Though Erasmus' book was later placed on the *Index* of the Inquisition's banned books, his early influence was felt through the humanities educational system of the Catholic elite of his day.[17]

In 1560, in the thick of the Tridentine reforms, Pius IV named his nephew Charles Borromeo to the post of cardinal and Archbishop of Milan at the age of twenty-two. This holy young man took seriously the Council's statement that preaching was to be the principal duty of bishops. He encouraged other bishops to preach. He began a renewal of preaching, creating preaching schools in his diocese. Catholics were ready for an alternative to thematic preaching. From his university humanistic education, Borromeo's approach to preaching was "shaped by his study of rhetoric and pagan ethics." Hence he continued and strengthened the moralistic emphasis of the Middle Ages via his rhetorical system: the proper content for preaching was to confront the congregation with "Sins, occasions of sins, virtues, and, finally the sacraments and other holy uses of the church."[18] His system was to set a pattern for the next four hundred years of preaching.

According to the Council of Trent, the purpose of preaching was: "teaching them the things which it is necessary for all to know unto salvation, and by announcing to them with briefness and plainness of discourse, the vices which they must avoid, and the virtues they must follow after, that they may escape everlasting punishment, and obtain the glory of heaven."[19] The focus of preaching, then, became what the faithful must know and do to get to heaven. The emphasis on works would spur many generations of Catholics toward the implicit preaching of social justice, through the building of hospitals, the education of schools, and care for the poor.

In the immediate aftermath of the Catholic Reformation, there were pockets of preaching fervor. Increasingly, though, to direct undue attention toward the skills of preaching and the Bible became suspect as being "too Protestant."[20] The practice did not follow the Tridentine decree of preaching as the primary duty of clergy. "Catholic preaching went in a very different direction. . . . Its preachers simply refused to move in the direction the Reformers moved in their reform of preaching."[21] For the next four hundred years, Catholic identity focused on the sacraments, painting a highly distinctive picture of what it meant "to be Catholic."

The "Manuals"

The conflict with Protestantism caused the Catholic Church to tighten its own ship. The proper training of clergy was mandated by the reforms of the Council of Trent, yet in the midst of the Wars of Religion, seminaries took a hundred years to get started in France. In the tightening, there was much caution: the Inquisition was reconstituted in 1542 to repress specific books and heretics. The bishops had increased powers to deal with nonconformist clerics. Orthodoxy was valued.

How was a preacher to teach good morals and right doctrine? The lower clergy used "how-to-do-it" manuals of homilies; preaching aids were expected, much as in the days of thematic preaching. Priests kept diaries of stories and illustration and metaphors that they copied from other how-to-manuals: the style of the sermon was a long string of these vignettes connected together. Such preaching was intended to be like a prose poem, though in practice it could get monotonous and a bit flabby: some were said to have gone on for an hour or more. Creativity was not encouraged.

In order to ensure that the faithful were instructed in right doctrine, in the next centuries, many dioceses issued preaching syllabi: curricula of what to preach and when to preach it. The content was to be the Ten Commandments, the Apostles' Creed, The Lord's Prayer, and an explanation of the sacraments. How to attain heaven and avoid hell were the topics to be directed toward the faithful to keep their morals pure.

How did the church view itself in terms of pulpit and pew? Pius X, in 1906, in his encyclical protesting the separation of church and state in France, stated that "the Church is an unequal society." The Catholic in the pew was poorly educated. The clergy were the professionally educated elite, held in high esteem. Thus, the "duty of the multitude is to allow themselves to be led."[22]

The ship remained steady, preaching right morals and right doctrine.[23] Spiritual movements came and went; wars brought down nations and changed territorial boundaries; religious orders were banned and then reinstated; the church spread into new mission territory; the Curia shrank protectively inward and then cautiously moved outward again; scientific advances changed the way that people saw the world. The purpose of preaching remained. The 1917 Code of Canon Law (#1347) declared: "In sacred sermons, there shall be set forth first of all those things that the faithful must believe and that which they ought to do for salvation."[24]

In the next century, secular culture was about to shift radically and quickly. The adequacy of the four-hundred-year-old prescription for preaching would come into question. The Catholic sermon/homily, which had stood so still for so long without much notice, was about to be bombarded and tossed from all sides—both from within the church and from without.

The Earth Quakes Outside the Church

In the first third of the twentieth century, the church was deeply concerned about the influence of Modernism on the faith of believers. Culturally, the modernist mindset questioned the time-tested traditions and certainties of religion. This is a well-researched phenomenon.

At the same time, the seeds of another cultural shift were quietly being planted. The rising disciplines of marketing and public relations (PR) have had at least as great an influence on Catholic faith as modernism but are not as well documented in religious circles. The turn toward the customer in marketing changed the playing field for all forms of communication in the twentieth century. Bethlehem Steel opened the very first public relations department in 1930; General Motors followed suit in 1931 and U.S. Steel in 1936.[25]

From out of this framework came the first (recorded) book on preaching which was written by a listener. O'Brien Atkinson, a writer of secular advertising, was more than seventy years old when he urged a homiletical turn toward the pew in 1942. His book, *How to Make Us Want Your Sermon: by a Listener,* was a one-of-a-kind primer on preaching for Roman Catholic priests.[26] Rather than writing about preaching from a "sender" perspective, Atkinson wrote as a lifelong "receiver" of preaching. He opened his preface:"This text is a plea for better understanding. It tries to bring to you the story of what happens to the words of your sermon after they leave your lips; a story that no one else is so well fitted to tell as the layman."[27] From his background, Atkinson provided what he saw as a clear example of why defining one's market and understanding the "customer" should matter to the "product" of preaching:

> A secular speaker asks himself, what should I say to this particular audience? An advertising man realizes that the woman who buys a fur coat and the farmer who buys paint for his cowshed have very different views, tastes, and motives. A $5000 advertisement might be wasted by appealing to such a woman in a way that would bring orders from thousands of farmers. Yet the clergyman often seems to take his audience for granted. He delivers a sermon that is not what the people need, but what he would like to say. Why?[28]

The accountability of a "seller" relied on discerning what his customer wanted so that he got the sale. If the customer refused the "company's" product, the seller was not effective. Atkinson offered a parallel of this interaction:

> You are to preach. You may be a curate or a cardinal. We are to listen. We may be a small town congregation or a vast multitude attending a Eucharistic world congress. In either case, and in every case, we have one advantage. Whoever you are, wherever you preach, however lowly or lofty the occasion, the prosperity of your sermon will rest with us. If we say it was over our heads, or hard to follow, or dull and wearisome, there will be no appeal from that verdict. You may think us stupid, and we may be stupid, but our verdict will be final.[29]

Atkinson pleaded for preachers to turn toward the listener at this early point in advertising history. Was he heard? No. Catholic sermons continued to be sender-side:"He delivers a sermon that is not what the people need, but what he would like to say." The lay street preacher had high hopes that the Sunday sermon would find a place in the listener's heart:"But the truth is that we want to listen. We are hopeful that your talk will interest us and hold us. And if you go about it the right way, you can interest us, and greatly help us . . . for we want to understand you . . . whenever your sermon speaks our language, deals with our spiritual troubles, raises our hopes, inspires us to carry on—we are truly grateful.[30]

It is seventy years since Atkinson wrote his little book on preaching. The field of consumer behavior has grown exponentially in its understanding of how listeners process and "buy into" messages and yet the church wonders, "Why does the secular world seem to be 'winning?'" There have been millions and millions of dollars poured into the quest to strengthen commitment and build loyalty toward a brand or a product so that those who are deeply committed will create "buzz" in the marketplace. (Think of the resonance created by brands such as Notre Dame football,[31] Apple computers, Harley-Davidson motorcycles.) By contrast, the field of Catholic homiletics has invested virtually nothing to understand what engenders commitment and loyalty. We operate from conjecture: preachers wonder and evangelization committees ask, but we do not have adequate data to understand what creates "buzz" through Sunday preaching. We may have seen it happen. We do not know why or how it does.[32]

Why is this history of consumer psychology important to the history of preaching in the twentieth century? It is a significant factor in forming the way listeners of today hear a homily. They expect the message to *try* to connect with them. It is now implicitly considered to be a sign of respect to take the respondent's needs into account when delivering a message. In American culture, it is a sign of disrespect for the sender to disregard the receiver.[33]

In addition, the elevation of personal choice and the allure of satisfaction through purchasing have changed cultural values which had once been considered timeless.[34] What can we do about secularism, individualism, and consumerism? At this point in history, we ourselves can work to be as effective as possible. The love, joy, peace, and fulfillment of the gospel of Jesus Christ is the most life-giving "product" out there. Passing on the faith is not magic. It takes work.

Before we turn to other recent historical factors that impact the little seven- to ten-minute talk at the Sunday liturgy from within the church, let us recap where we have been. Each of the historical eras still linger around today's homily: the grammarian's explication of Origen, the rhetorical emphasis of Augustine, the thematic preaching of the mendicants, the catechetical teaching of the missionaries, the moralizing and doctrinal preaching of the post-Tridentine church. If these eras were strains of music, their melodies still play in the Catholic world. Some of the current-day tug-and-pull in the expectations for the homily comes from these historical factors.

In the early twentieth century the sermon was not mandatory; it was unrelated to the Scriptures that were read at Mass and it was often set apart from the eucharistic liturgy itself. It took a gathering of cardinals, theologians, and bishops to gather in Rome from 1962 to 1965 to lift the battered and bruised Sunday homily to the top of the pile of bricks under which it had been buried.

The Homily Joins the Divine Liturgy

Those who lived before the Second Vatican Council tell stories of parish life which was immersed in a Catholic culture—nuns and priests were revered but also interacted as friends of the family. Little is recalled of preaching; moral absolutes dominated Catholic life, such as chastity and the sanctity of marriage, use your envelope, don't miss Mass, self-sacrifice ("offer it up"), avoid sin, strive for heaven, and stay out of hell. Fulton Sheen was the superstar preacher/teacher on TV. The clergy were the church, and the people let them "do" it.

Anecdotes about parish life just after Vatican II tell of: changes in the liturgy; priests and nuns leaving or changing clothes (or names); new musical instruments and styles of singing; parish councils where the laypeople were supposed to help Father; and the Mass in English with the altar turned around. They don't mention the homily. Why not? Vatican II made two significant changes to homilies: (1) it is to be an integral part of the liturgy;[35] and (2) it should focus on Scripture (leaving some room for doctrine). Though this was a shift, it was not as earth-shaking as so many of the other moves. The Council only gave a bare-bones hint of what the restored homily should look like.[36]

One of the monumental shifts of Vatican II was the change in belief about who was to be "church." The "we" of the clergy as church (as Pius X had described in 1906) shifted to "the people of God." Who was to proclaim the gospel to the world? Pulpit and pew were to work together for the glory of God with distinct roles but a common mission. The passivity of the laity was gone. Laypeople were to be co-responsible: "every man and woman may share in the saving work of redemption . . . no member is purely passive: sharing in the life of the body each member also shares in its activity."[37]

In his 1975 apostolic exhortation Evangelization in the Modern World (*Evangelii Nuntiandi*), Paul VI laid out a clear description of his hopes for the homily as integral to evangelization. The homily "has a particular role in evangelization . . . it expresses the profound faith of the sacred minister and is deeply imbued with love . . . it will always be a privileged occasion for communicating the word of the Lord."[38] Focus on the homily began to grow. Expectations for the homily began to grow.

Never before had a homily been required at Mass. Remember the bishop preaching at the cathedrals? Now every Fr. Tom, Fr. Dick, and Fr. Harry had to preach at all of the Masses, even daily ones, as well as funerals and weddings. Most of the clergy had little training in public speaking. Scripture had not been a large part of their pre-Vatican II seminary curriculum. In this new expectation for preaching, where were priests to turn for direction? Since the Council recommended scriptural preaching, the natural place to turn was to the Protestant homiletic world. How, then, were priests to translate that for a Catholic congregation? What was the Catholic vision of the restored homily?

The U.S. church took a leading role in beginning to unpack that question. Our Catholic bishops gave a carefully crafted answer in their 1982 USCCB document *Fulfilled in your Hearing*: the homily is liturgical; it is to take the concerns of the assembly to heart; the document outlines how to prepare well; it encourages the use of Scripture as a lens for the interpretation of life. The number of Catholic books on preaching is still small but increasing; many come from the United States. The only Catholic graduate school in the world that offers a doctorate in preaching, Aquinas Institute, is in St. Louis. Among the nations of the world, the United States is a homiletical hot spot.

> Why is Catholic preaching such an uphill climb? Let us be patient: the history behind us is weighty and change in the church takes time. Let us also be impatient: time solves nothing if we do nothing with it.

Why is Catholic preaching such an uphill climb? It is surrounded by its history. Christian preaching was honored and celebrated for its first fifteen hundred years. Then for four hundred more years, it was tucked away into a corner, overpowered by other liturgical elements that more strongly formed Catholic identity. For the past thirty years in the United States, that little string of words has received more attention, though perhaps less than it deserves.

We are still early in this era of the reinvigoration of preaching. Let us be patient: the history behind us is weighty and change in the church takes time. Let us also be impatient: time solves nothing if we do nothing with it.

An Era for Preaching?

Today, we live in an age of communication. We have more resources than ever before: At the touch of a finger, we can access the homilies of St.

John Chrysostom, Bernard of Clairvaux and Pope Francis. We have more understanding than ever before: the scriptural background for a Johannine pericope is readily available in books and articles and blogs. We can pray evening prayer anywhere and at anytime: the Liturgy of the Hours comes along in our smartphones. A homily can be typed on a tablet at a picnic table under a tree. We can speak into a microphone, and a computer program will type out those spoken words. We can videotape a homily and broadcast it all over the world through the internet.

We live in a connected world. That is our opportunity. With a concentration of efforts and resources, with all that we have available at our fingertips, Catholic Sunday preaching could make a major impact on future history. That is our hope for preaching the Good News.

We live in a connected world. That is also our challenge. In the early church, the community was the source of authority. After the printing press, the written Word took cultural precedence over the authority of the community. Now with the connections of cyberspace, as one youth said, "You can always find another spin on the internet." Where will that mindset take us? What will be the new source of authority?

We are at yet another turning point in history. How can a preacher speak a credible word to the people of today? What are the challenges that preachers face in crafting a connected and convincing homily? We turn to them and ask them, in this next chapter.

Applications for Preachers from the Greats of History

1. Gregory of Nyssa: Be a careful observer of life; know how your people live and feel.

2. Origen: Build the flock, morally and spiritually.

3. Chrysostom: Never stop improving; preaching is a skill to be learned and practiced.

4. Augustine: Be a person of depth. "He had such an enormous amount to say."

5. Francis of Assisi: Be simple. Love God.

6. Dominic: Be learned. Take the preaching task seriously.

7. Ignatius: See God in all things.

8. Paul VI: Preaching is a privileged occasion within the liturgy.

9. Atkinson: Fit the preaching to the needs of the people.

10. Benedict XVI: The quality of homilies needs to be improved.

Painting a Picture of God

I am the good shepherd. I know my own and my own know me, just as the Father knows me and I know the Father. And I lay down my life for the sheep. (John 10:14–15)

It was June, the time when many clergy change assignments. For the interview, we sat in the midst of packing boxes, for Fr. [D] was moving to another town.[1] The summer sun streamed in through the window as we talked. This experienced pastor described his core concern for "connection" with his people:

> Fr. [D]: I'm a social creature by habit . . .walking through the church with great reverence before a Mass and I pause and will tap someone and say, "What's your name?" Or I'll see someone that I already remember their name. I have found over the years that is what I love church to be about. People are always attracted to the priest, [thinking], "Ah! The priest knows my name." . . . I just want people to realize they should be doing this with one another; so you know who is sitting next to you; someone sitting next to you could have had a death in the family last week and you know they are emotionally hurt and they are here and wouldn't it be nice if someone else knew that? Get to know the community. I do an awful lot of that work before Mass, after Mass, chitchatting with people even if I don't have the Mass. I'm psyched and it creates a feeling—they love their priest and "it's good to go to this church."
>
> Interviewer: And the priest loves them.
>
> Fr. [D]: Yes, that's the truth.

I asked how that translated to his preaching:

Fr. [D]: If I get them in friendship, then if you really have a message, they're going to know me and they're going to listen; it's
getting them first to pay attention, and they pay attention to
their friend. *(starts to chuckle)* If I came across without knowing
them and with some authority, that could work too . . . if I was
an excellent preacher and captivated them with every verb and
adjective imaginable.

Social and relational connections came to mind first for this priest. A
younger priest, Fr. [E] saw connection as more homiletically content-
based: "I think part of the job as a preacher is to do this exposition or this
revelation or disclosure of things that they already know (at least here in
their heads) and let it sink to the heart and it blows open and that's where
conversion takes place . . . that has been my experience anyway."

   Though they travel two different pathways in relating to their people,
both of these men are preachers who connect well. The people in the
pew hunger for that authentic connection. A sophomore from New York
said, "When a preacher connects with me it means that God himself is
connecting with me." A fifteen-year-old girl from Maine asked for the
homilist, "To be able to show you the face of God."

Preacher as Icon

   What does it mean to show someone "the face of God?" As the two
priests "on-the-ground" described, to care about their people meant to
continually strive to be a man who connected with them—both by person
and by message. This imi-
tates the priestly ministry of
Jesus Christ himself.

   Priestly identity which
leads to priestly service is
at the core of clergy life:
"Priestly ordination is a
radical, total reordering of

> To care about the people means to continually strive to be a man who connects with them—both by person and by message. This imitates the priestly ministry of Jesus Christ himself.

a man in the eyes of God and his Church, bringing about an identity of
ontological 'reconfigurement' with Christ."[2] His way of life is integral to
his service.

   Preaching the Mystery of Faith lays out four identity/service themes spe-
cifically geared toward the ministry of preaching.[3] A priest is to be a man
of holiness; through prayer, "the true pastor and good shepherd knows his

people's sorrows, their anxieties, their weaknesses, their capacity for love, their abiding joys, and their deepest longings." He is to be a man of Scripture; if he has personally encountered God in the Scriptures and "sees the world through biblical eyes," then his preaching will impart a scriptural lens to his people's deepest longings. He is to be a man of Tradition; if his life is imbued with the richness of "theology, spirituality, the liturgy, the lives of the saints, the formal teaching of the Church, great Catholic art, architecture, and poetry," his preaching will draw from a deep theological well. He is to be a man of communion, of mission, and dialogue; his preaching thus honors and names the experience of the people whom he serves. The preacher and his preaching task flow seamlessly together. Plumbing his spiritual depths, like Augustine, a really fine preacher has a lot to say and a lot to give.

> "Within the Church's life the priest is a man of communion, in his relations with all people he must be a man of mission and dialogue. Deeply rooted in the truth and charity of Christ, and impelled by the desire and imperative to proclaim Christ's salvation to all, the priest is called to witness in all his relationships to fraternity, service and a common quest for the truth, as well as a concern for the promotion of justice and peace."
>
> —Blessed John Paul II, *Pastores Dabo Vobis* (I Will Give You Shepherds), 18

> "[P]eople appreciate pastors and preachers who cultivate personal relationships with them and demonstrate a willingness to move beyond their comfort zones and enter the world of the 'other.'"
>
> —*Preaching the Mystery of Faith*, 39

Building upon this identity, the proclamation of the word of God is then the primary task of priests: "and rightfully they (the laity) expect this from their priests. Since no one can be saved who does not first believe, priests, as co-workers with their bishops, have the primary duty of proclaiming the Gospel of God to all. In this way they fulfill the command of the Lord: 'Going therefore into the whole world to preach the Gospel to every creature' (Mk 16:15), and they establish and build up the People of God."[4]

If the preacher walks in solidarity with his people, then the Holy Spirit who is the Great Connector—who wants to be here, wants to be at work, and wants to unite us—will speak through him. Ideally, in the preaching event, a priest paints an icon by how he invests his life, composes his words, and bodily expresses them. The receivers then communally enter into that preaching event; through that window of Word and words, they encounter God. The-Inaudible-the-Invisible is thus revealed through the audible and visible homiletic event.

Spiritual Formation + Homiletical Skill = Holy Preaching

In the past twenty years, our Catholic seminaries have focused on forming men who are good shepherds.[5] From the responses of my 561 young friends in the pew, findings suggest that we are doing well in that formation: those who attend Mass regularly rated "the person of the preacher" very highly: 93 percent agreed that he exuded a love for Jesus; 91 percent can say that he is "friendly to me." Laypeople respect their parish priests highly.[6] As the pastor said in the opening quote to this chapter, they love their priests and their priests love them. Our efforts in formation have borne fruit.

From the outsider perspective of these young listeners, we are developing good men.[7] Those on the inside may castigate themselves about becoming holier (not unlike a family dynamic), but laypeople suggest that the challenge centers more on the homiletical skills of content and delivery. I discussed these findings with Archbishop Joseph Kurtz of Louisville. I offered him the formula, "spiritual formation + homiletical skill = holy preaching." He made the insightful comment that we are doing better in the more difficult half of the equation. Humbly he added, "though all our efforts, beginning with myself, to grow more deeply in spiritual formation . . . in the grace of Jesus Christ . . . , will never reach a point on this earth at which we can safely say: 'I have arrived!'"[8]

Spiritual Formation for Preaching

When listeners look at their preacher, what do they see? Augustine believed that the "life of the speaker has greater weight in determining whether he is obediently heard than any grandness of eloquence."[9] The source of the message plays a role in facilitating the encounter of the receiver. From this study and from others, the vast majority of the "guys" are good-hearted and well-intentioned men. Of the youth who attend Mass regularly in my study, 82 percent agreed or strongly agreed that their homilist was a positive role model for them. Some even raved about them: "I have had a deacon that has really connected with me. He always greets me with a hug or a smile. He calls me by name and always asks what's going on in my life. Even though he is friends with my parents, I feel that he genuinely cares about *me*. When he preaches, he'll make eye contact with me and that makes me feel like he is genuinely talking to me."

If the preaching event is iconic, then the preacher cannot get out of the way. As the bishops' document delineates, he *is* the way: a man of holiness, Scripture, Tradition, and communion. The person of the preacher matters. The icon should be painted as beautifully as possible.

Developing Homiletical Skills

Formation takes years and, as Archbishop Kurtz commented, is never done. Prayer and holiness are central to preaching effectiveness and growth there is certainly welcome. Yet according to young listeners, from two different sources of measurement, thirty to forty percent of the preachers whom they evaluated were lacking elements that are taught in an introductory oral communications class: make one point, speak clearly, and do not repeat yourself or ramble. Listeners asked: apply the gospel to my life, help me with my problems, relate to me, and let me relate to you. Those requests were consistent no matter the age of the homilist or the faith level of the listener. Adults in the pew have said the same.[10]

Our needs in preaching are not so insurmountable. Communication skills are highly teachable. Thus, a focus on basic homiletical skills in the next twenty years could bear fruit in the same way that the focus on spiritual formation has borne fruit in the past twenty years.

Growth in Homiletical Skill is Integral to Priestly Identity

To be ordained into the person of Christ is a high calling. Integral to priestly identity is the willingness and the humility to never stop growing. In love for his people, a priest hungers to bring them into an encounter with God through his person and through his message. Therefore, growth in homiletical skill is integral to priestly identity. Ministerial service is not tacked on to priestly identity but intrinsic to it. In *Pastores Dabo Vobis*, Pope John Paul II speaks of growth within that calling: "Ongoing formation helps the priest to be and *act* as a priest in the spirit and style of Jesus the Good Shepherd."[11] "To be" and "to act" flow together: "Integration is at the heart of ongoing formation, as priests grow in bringing together *who* they are and *what* they do."[12] The homily is a key integrating moment for priestly ministry. One is never done maturing: "Given the importance of the preaching ministry for the life and mission of the Church, it is not a surprise that becoming an effective homilist capable of bringing the message of Scriptures into the life of the Christian community is a life-long and demanding process."[13]

Clergy Concerns in Preaching

As we continue to unpack the complexities that surround the homily, what do clergy "on the ground" have to say about the world that surrounds that little seven- to ten-minute string of words at a Sunday liturgy? What are the tugs and pulls in their lives concerning Sunday preaching?

Weary beyond Weary

Many of our clergy are tired. I was giving a talk at a district meeting soon after *Preaching the Mystery of Faith* was made public. I asked if any of the men had read it. One pastor raised his hand and told the group, "If you think you are tired now, read that document. Then you will *really* be weary."

The ideal of knowing the people, appropriating art and poetry and spirituality and Scripture study and the languages of diverse people and then incorporating theology and catechesis and Scripture in the midst of a sixty-hour week of administration and hospital visits and parish meetings and weddings and funerals and fitting it all into a talk at one of many Masses . . . was overwhelming. From the priest's expression, he looked like a truckload of bricks had been dumped onto *his* head. He felt a disconnection between the written vision and concrete parish reality. Another priest described the disconnection this way: "The people 'downtown' don't understand us. . . ."

One pastor, Fr. [F], had been in his position for three years. He described his preaching week:

> I had four funerals this week and daily Mass: two Masses on Monday, two daily Masses. And I preach at least once a day, sometimes twice a day, and sometimes three times a day. Last Friday, I preached four times . . . I imagine after a while I become less effective when I do that.

A priest friend had emailed to me about "the overwhelmingly busy schedules of overworked men who are, collectively, getting older every year." When I commented to Fr. [F] that a lot of priests feel time-pressured, he responded, "Very much so." He said that he had more time in the fifteen years that he had been an associate in a parish.[14] He talked about his new role as pastor:

> It is just really hard and it's unrealistic what is asked of priests. . . .
> The things that would help us to remain on top of our field and
> stay engaged? It's just on top of everything else . . . I think a
> number would love to do it [take the time for continuing educa-
> tion in preaching], but they wonder "How can I find the time" or
> "Where will I find the energy for it?" because we're aging. I get
> tired. I was thinking about this the other day. Fifteen years ago,
> I wouldn't have felt as tired as I did on that particular day after
> all the running around I did. But the years catch up after awhile.

The average age of Catholic priests is sixty-three years old.[15] As Fr. [F] described, he doesn't have the same energy that he did when he was younger. Time also affects his ability to prepare: "I don't have as much time to prepare as I would like. I used to have more time before I was a pastor. I would like to have more time to think about what I want to say, pray about it, so it's not just what I want to say but what does God want me to say. Preaching everyday gets to be a burden."

Parishioners do not see the many emergencies that clergy deal with. An unseen weariness also comes from the continually-on-call nature of priestly life. One man shared with me a story of praying and holding the hand of a driver under the sixteen wheels of a jackknifed semi-truck as he watched the man die. Another spoke of being called by the police to a basement splattered with blood where a man had blown his brains out, as if a priest can give "last rites" to a man already gone. The image of baptizing a twelve-ounce premature baby at two in the morning, the anguish of the parents at that loss, and the sorrow of the hospital staff who had worked so hard to save that baby—these are images that never leave one's head. Especially when a man has just been ordained, these painful experiences weigh heavily on his heart, yet ministering to people in their crisis moments is also moving and supplies deep meaning to priestly life.

Some of the fatigue comes from other worries and concerns. One priest shared, "A lot of discouragement too, especially among those who thought they saw in Vatican II the promise of a different way of being church and being priests . . . and the sexual abuse scandal . . . many guys are just feeling beaten to death." Experienced clergy have seen programs come and go, beginning with great enthusiasm and then dying a slow death, especially in the aftermath of Vatican II. That makes them cautious of anything that looks "gimmicky" or "trendy." The question is, "Will this last?" Some older clergy feel a bit jaded from thirty years of always trying "something new."

Fewer men also shoulder more responsibilities. More live alone. There is a growing dichotomy of cultural experience between preachers and their congregations. Communication modes are changing and clergy wonder: can preaching continue to be an effective medium? As priests age, their people are still young. Preachers and/or parishioners also increasingly come from other countries, with hurdles of language and cultural differences.

There is never an end to the good that can be done in ministry and the men with whom I talked were doing much good. One younger pastor, in his forties, said, "I'm tired. But it's a good tired. Do you know what I mean?" I did. At the same time as finding their ministry challenging, the majority of priests also find it highly rewarding.[16]

Just Not a Priority

Where does Sunday preaching fit into the overall picture? In conversations with clergy, some of them imply that it is just not a priority for them. Why? To preach may not why they entered the priesthood.[17] Perceptions vary: "I do it well enough to get by"; "it does not really depend on me"; "I have so many other things to do"; and "I am not an entertainer." Priests spend the least amount of time preparing their Sunday homily when compared to other responsibilities.[18] With so many things to do, getting a homily ready for Sunday is important, but it is not the highest of priorities. In *The Great American Sermon Survey,* Carrell found the same—17 percent of the Catholic preachers she surveyed considered "sermon prep" to be their most important task (in contrast to 47 percent of Protestant clergy). From her results, seventy-five percent of those who admitted to "winging" their Sunday talk were Catholic preachers.[19]

In one of my clergy interviews, when asked to rate (on a scale of 1 to 10) how important his homily preparation was in terms of the use of his time, one pastor shrugged, "Somewhere about a 5." When asked how his people would rate it, he leaned back and then chuckled, "Oh, probably about a 9!" On the recording, his laughter pealed out when I told him that he had nailed the response of young parishioners almost exactly: in a focus group, when averaged, they had responded a 9.5.

In sacramental theology, effectiveness is not based on the holiness or personality of the minister but on Christ himself as the author of those sacraments (*ex opere operato*). Atkinson, the 1942 lay street preacher, wondered if *ex opere operato* trickled into attitudes toward preaching and thus leaked into the homiletic message. With a whimsical sense of humor, he questioned whether the preacher feels assured of the help of the Holy Spirit, suggesting, "The sermon, however is not self-acting. And the evidence is that the Holy Ghost doesn't do a great deal for those who expect Him to carry the [whole] load."[20]

Young listeners' antennae are keenly attuned to lack of preparation. They evaluate public speaking from their classmates at school all the time, thus they are attuned to slipshod preparation. One said, "Do [your] homework and be prepared."

The lack of the priority of preaching reveals itself institutionally also, especially in relation to youth. In the youth ministry document, *Renewing the Vision*, preaching is buried within a subsection about prayer and worship on page 46.[21] The National Initiative for Adolescent Catechesis (NIAC), in seeking to reinvigorate the discipling of young people, does not discuss the influence of Sunday preaching.[22] In the *General Directory for Catechesis*, the homily is mentioned in the context of the Ministry of the Word for Catholic school Masses and in its role as adult formation.[23] In the entire working document for the bishops' world synod on evangelization in October 2012, there are two sentences on Sunday preaching (neither in relation to youth). The significance of the homily to discipleship, especially of youth, is a serious blind spot in our documents.

If it seems that our preachers and the institutional church are not prioritizing the efforts to foster homiletical skill-sets, especially in relation to connecting with their children and their youth, laypeople are left to wonder why. In the words of young people themselves, that seven- to ten-minute string of words within the Sunday liturgy makes a significant impact on whether they stay or they go.

In order to pass on the other insights from the youth in my survey, I asked a second set of questions in my clergy interviews that centered around effective ways to help homilists to grow. Starting with feedback and interaction concerns, we discussed ways to keep preaching fresh, materials that homilists use for insight, and ways to foster growth through continuing education. These men had much to say and were grateful to be asked.

Preaching Improvement

As mentioned in the introduction about the Loud Silence, on the local level, constructive and helpful interaction between the pulpit and the pew is virtually nonexistent. One pastor said, "98 percent of the time, there is no feedback from the people in the pew . . . No, wait . . . maybe that number is too low—we NEVER get feedback from people in the pew." One man said that he regularly asks, so he gets some responses. Another said that he had received two written notes in the past two years at the parish; he was grateful for that. Shea describes it this way: "Most of us tend to preach in a vacuum where we are forced to assess our own preaching and draw conclusions using the few tidbits of input that we only casually and informally receive. We preach without the benefit of concrete feedback that could make a radical difference in what and how we preach."[24]

Unaware of the Impact of the Homily

When laypeople begin to speak about the influence of the homily in their lives, clergy are often surprised. Preaching is, of course, not the only factor in the system of faith growth, but its impact appears to be a substantial one, more important than most Catholic preachers realize. When preaching into a vacuum of feedback; when no one says anything; when "Good homily, Father" with a handshake at the door is all that a preacher hears (even if he did not preach that day), the implication is that the homily does not matter all that much.

By contrast, feedback does come from being part of significant moments in people's lives. When a priest has anointed her dying husband, a widow has a gleam of gratitude in her eye that never leaves. Twenty years later, a young man will say with satisfaction, "Deacon, you baptized me." At a sixtieth anniversary, a couple will tell back-in-the-day stories about "Monsignor," now long deceased. These comments tell of that moment's significance. Clergy find these experiences rewarding.

Perhaps gratitude for the day-in-and-day-out homily is like thanking Mom for the continual sustenance of her oatmeal rather than for Thanksgiving dinner. When clergy never hear that the bread and butter of preaching nourishes, that "what you are saying and how you say it matters to us," they do not realize how much impact their seven- to ten-minute homily has in the life of their people. The homiletic reward system is out of order.

We Are Above Average

Perception about the need for improvement can also affect a homilist's willingness to participate in preaching improvement. The unevenness of feedback may paint an unrealistically rosy picture of one's own preaching. Both Lovrick and Shea found in independent surveys that 82 percent of the priests surveyed considered themselves to be above average or excellent in

---

Tough questions for tough times

(For personal evaluation for a preacher)

1. How do your people see you? Your message?
2. On a scale of one to ten, how much does your homily preparation matter in terms of your time commitments? How much do you think that it matters to your people?
3. What is going on in the minds of your hearers when you are preaching? What will they already give you?
4. When a person in your pew thinks of people of deep faith, are you among the top ten that he or she thinks about?
5. When a young man is considering his vocation in life, do you stand out as a vibrant representative for what he aspires to be?
6. What image springs to mind when your people hear your name? Are there any obstacles that pop up when they hear your name?
7. Do you have a reputation for treating your people with caring, kindness, and love? What memories of "church" and "priest, deacon, or bishop" do you give them?
8. Is your preaching creating "buzz" in your local community (of an uplifting kind)? What do your people value most in your preaching?

---

their preaching.[25] Shea suggests that this may impact their perception of their need for improvement: "Eighty-two percent of all priests rate their preaching as being above average versus the preaching of all other priests. Since the self-assessment of preaching is so favorable, it could explain why so few priests are prepared to invest the effort and time to improve their preaching."[26]

This data would suggest that at a round table of ten priests sitting down to a dinner, at least three of the men are sadly mistaken about their homiletical abilities. Without consistent conversation and objective assessment, preachers work from assumption and highly imbalanced feedback.

Spiritual Growth Is a Challenge

What do clergy think about each other's homilies? One man said, "We almost never hear anyone else preach." Vacation time is one of the few opportunities to hear another preacher speak at Mass. What do they think when they do hear it? Not much: shallowness of the message and delivery problems stand out. From the priests who responded to Lovrick's survey in Toronto, 55 percent felt that "superficial content" was one of the top two problems in the homilies that they heard from others; "flat, boring delivery" was the other.[27] Lovrick quoted a seminarian: "I recently heard a homily that remained on the surface, and I was intrigued by some of the person's imagery and selection of language, among other things, but what I found lacking was depth. When I realized that it wasn't going anywhere, I just wanted it to end. That I am guilty of this is one of my greatest preaching fears."[28]

Role models for effective preaching are also missing, especially among those who work solo and for those who minister in many parishes. Several years ago, I sat next to a young priest at a seminar. He called himself a "circuit rider": each weekend he administered the sacraments to five parishes in the rural South. As we began to talk about preaching, he said that he could not remember the last time that he had heard someone else preach. He was getting tired of hearing himself talk. Working hard just to keep his head above water, what he missed most from his (rather recent) seminary days was the time to pray and study. After ordination, time for prayer and spiritual enrichment were the first things that had gone out of the window. Reading, study, and going to workshops was a dream for another lifetime.

"If we didn't get it in the seminary, it is not likely to happen," said one pastor. "Change is difficult for a priest." Continuing education is not required for clergy as it is in other professions. I asked a traveling mission priest if he understood why homily content is weak. He said that he stayed in rectories week after week and saw, "The magazines don't move." Valuable reading material sat on the coffee table on Thursday in the same place that it had been on the previous Saturday. This was consistent across the country. "Our men don't read" was his explanation for the lack of depth in Catholic preaching.[29] Another priest agreed that flatness leaked into the homilies; he concluded his interview with a sigh, "We need a renewal."

Isolation and Cultural Disparity

The lack of feedback and spiritual enrichment also reflects a broader cultural reality. There are some preachers who also live and speak in isolation. One pastor lamented that he had never been invited to dinner, to a graduation party, or to a birthday party. His parishioners kept him on a pedestal as "Father . . . a priest, a man in a robe," not as a human being who needed friendship and contact. How was he supposed to know how his people lived? The closest that he got to interaction was when he wandered down the street and talked to a little boy who ran a lemonade stand. He himself wondered, how could he possibly relate to them? He did not know how they lived. He was interested in making stronger connections with his people in his preaching, but he simply did not know how to do it: "We tend to live in a bubble" was how another priest described it. Lack of knowledge of how the "other" lives makes the connection of preaching much more difficult.

Getting There Is a Challenge

Accessibility is also a concern in ongoing formation. Lovrick found that 70 percent of the preachers who responded to his survey in Canada were at least somewhat willing to participate in preaching improvement workshops or seminars, but they had to travel long hours to do so.[30] Access to continuing education experiences can become an issue of the best use of limited time. One whom I interviewed described his experience of workshops as a waste of hours: the trip to the seminary (and back) ate up 138 minutes when traffic was good, in addition to the three hours for the talk. He found it more rewarding to use that time to visit with parishioners in the hospital.

Keep It Concrete

Preachers asked for practicality in the ongoing formation that they get in homiletics. After a weeklong course in preaching, one pastor observed that he had spent five days talking and learning about preaching, and then on Friday evening, he had to go home and prepare his homily. Might it not have been more fruitful to create the Sunday homily together in the process of the preaching course? Preachers who come to homiletic workshops would prefer to go home with something in hand. Another preacher suggested sending him a short email about preaching every week. "Keep it simple," he said. Rather than theory, they preferred to apply their learning, asking, "How does this help my preaching?"

The world of the homily in the life of clergy "on the ground" is complex. Their concerns will not be addressed by attending one workshop. To help them out, we have to be aware of their hopes and struggles to preach well and thus design methods of ongoing formation that meet their concrete needs. Laypeople would like to help with that. At the same time, we have to recognize that we do not work out of the same roles or the same sets of experiences.

Co-cultures Running in Parallel

When Lori Carrell conducted her listener study of Catholic and Protestant preachers in the *Great American Sermon Survey*, she found that two "co-cultures" ran in parallel:[31] "When it comes to perceptions about the sermon [or homily], preachers have much more in common with each other than they do with their listeners. Preachers read the same books, experience the same preparation challenges, have the same occupational stresses, and may talk to each other about preaching from a 'sender' approach. Listeners share the experience of listening to sermons week after week. Listeners talk to listeners about sermons. Our perceptions are therefore reinforced by our own 'co-cultures.'"[32] Fr. [T] spoke similarly about the disconnection between clergy and lay lives:

> My folks had priests over fairly often at my house [fifty years ago], so I was able to feel more comfortable than maybe your typical Catholic kid would. . . . I think that if you have a priest that seems human to you, [it helps]. . . . Most kids don't get much exposure to a priest and so the priesthood is a mystery to them. And it is certainly a mystery to their parents because their parents don't connect to the priest either. In a way, we are a strange beast to a lot of our parishioners . . .

In his childhood, to invite the priests over was a more common experience. As a "strange beast, he says that now,

> I have not been invited to many people's homes here (at his new parish). . . , but . . . I've never been in a parish where that was a real common thing. Typically. . .I've been with at least one other priest, and I can't say that the priests I've lived with were out all the time because they were being invited to peoples' homes. . . . The [people themselves] don't know it's a nice thing to do, it doesn't occur to them or maybe they never grew up with that as an experience, so they don't even consider it as an option.

This lack of conversation and interaction can isolate clergy from lay life. Like Fr. [D] in the opening to this chapter, the relational/social elements may have to be intentionally cultivated. In more interactive parish cultures, clergy can find themselves running ragged with invitations to graduation parties, golfing outings, and First Communion celebrations. Even there, though, lay life is likely to be presented at its most sanitized. Rarely is a priest exposed to the bellowing of "Get in the car!" that happens ten minutes before a family demurely slides into the pew.[33]

The increase of international priests in American parishes has been a great blessing to the church in the United States. It also presents a unique cultural conundrum. Language disparities, different underlying childhood experiences, and an alternate perspective on life may both enrich and hinder the ability to connect with the people in the pew. Many shepherds from foreign lands emanate an enthusiasm for God that is refreshing and contagious: with some inculturation, they can fashion that joy into the words and images that effectively enflame the flock.

In addition to clergy and lay life running in parallel in parish life, seminary formation focuses on fostering a common priestly identity as "brothers in Christ." Theoretical formation for the priesthood has historically weighed heavily: courses on theology, Scripture, liturgy and sacraments, and prayer are substantial and central to priestly identity. Skill-based training has always taken a back seat in the proportion of seminary courses allotted. One leader in homiletics described this process as "We are forming academically good men." Seminary culture, like any group that hangs together for long periods of time, has its own leveling—people start to talk alike, think alike, dress alike. . . . As in any group, you can tell an outsider because they don't look or think the same. We tend to be most influenced by those who are most like us.[34]

Does this theoretical training prepare seminarians to connect to the world to which they will be ministering after ordination? Manuel Flores, SJ, in an article in *America* magazine, echoed the propensity toward the theoretical in his comments about the implementation of the vision of the Second Vatican Council:

> The problem was not our vision of church but rather how to make it happen. The architectural blueprint, the picture, was there; but we had not mastered the engineering. Most priests learned about ministry by trial and error, by learning from experience. In our seminaries, we got an "architecture" or theological vision, but very little on the building of that vision. You have to do that on your own. That is a very costly way to learn, costly to people's faith.[35]

Learning the skills of ministry by trial and error is a "costly way to learn." Fortunately pastoral field education and courses in counseling and homiletics have increased in importance in our seminaries. How to balance the proportion of theological education with spiritual formation and the training for ministerial skill in an already overcrowded curriculum is an ongoing debate.[36]

Richard Stern asked laypeople to assess the homilies of seminarians who were about to be ordained. From their comments and from observations by faculty members, this "co-culture" was also present in his seminary setting at St. Meinrad: "There was still work to do in the area of adaptation to a parish-based hearer. . . . Illustrations were not parish-oriented. Respondents desired more of a connection to their daily experience."[37] Preaching styles that had been modeled by faculty in the school chapel tended to be academic and dry. The laity preferred more fire and more energy. From the lay feedback given to his graduating preachers, Stern suggested that the teaching of seminarians adapt to target preaching toward a more parish-oriented setting.[38]

If priestly and lay cultures run side by side—different priorities, different lenses, different experiences, different language—how do we connect pulpit and pew for the glory of God? We are not called to the same roles in the church; to "connect" does not mean to wash away clergy and lay differences. To walk toward God together in faith, the two parallel cultures have to find points of intersection to develop the closeness needed to preach well. The shepherd has to know his sheep. Pope Francis speaks of this proximity in an October 2013 interview, "The homily is the touchstone to measure the pastor's proximity and ability to meet his people, because those who preach must recognize the heart of their community and must be able to see where the desire for God is lively and ardent."[39]

What Are We Not Seeing?

We have a perception gap in how the two cultures view the importance of Sunday preaching. In the balance, for the lay world, the homily weighs heavily; for the clergy world, not so much. As this chapter has described: there are so many other things to do; there is no feedback or accountability; there is not an accurate perception of how it is going; the rewards system is broken; the sacraments matter more; there's no time. . . . But in the overall picture, perhaps the difference is *how* we see.

The sacrament of ordination, in which a man is ontologically changed into the person of Christ, transforms a man's identity. To be Christ to the world is a sacred responsibility. Priestly identity becomes his fundamental lens, his way of seeing the world.

Laypeople live in a skill-based world. Catholic priestly identity is not even within the scope of their imagination. Rather, they observe the outer

---

Summary of Clergy Concerns about Preaching

- Time-pressured. Many pastors are weary. Not as much time for homily preparation as they would like.

- Preaching is just not a priority; there are so many other things to do; many homilies are given in a week.

- Do not realize how much impact their 7- to 10-minute homily has in the faith life of their people.

- A cultural silence in feedback, assessment, and accountability, both from listeners, superiors, and those trained in communication. As a result, it is not clear how they are doing.

- May not feel a need to improve; the preaching is good enough. (82 percent consider themselves to be above average.)

- Do not know exactly how to improve, how better to relate to the people, especially the young. Rarely hear others preach or have role models for preaching.

- Preaching improvement programs are not accessible, especially in relation to time constraints.

- Continuing education has to be practical to make the best use of limited time.

---

expressions of what a priest or deacon or bishop does as he communicates the gospel. In evaluating preaching, laypeople ask, "Is this working?" When they see family and/or friends walk away, they conclude, "No."

For preaching to be effective in bringing people into an encounter with God, we need a healthy balance between formation and skill. When one side is overweighted, the church loses ground.

In excess, a cleric can become so encapsulated in his priestly identity that he lives in a bubble of self-satisfaction and self-protection and thus grows deaf to the cry of the laity to develop homiletical, pastoral, and relational skills. When he exclusively interacts with his brothers in faith and the inner circle of the parish; when he only thinks and talks about "churchy" things; when he exalts and protects his priestly turf at all costs; then he becomes what Pope Francis calls "narcissistic" and "clerically self-referential."

At the other extreme, laypeople can become so encapsulated in their identity as skill-based, results-focused, and success-oriented people that they in turn can live in a bubble of worldly-valued effectiveness. As a result, they grow blind to the call for spiritual formation to develop a personal relationship with God. When they only see the church through a secular lens; when they dismiss it for its lack of marketing, its weak institutional positioning, and its dearth of effective communications and strategic planning; they lose sight that there is something more at work here than what can be measured and analyzed.

We can clearly see the weakness of "the other side." How accurately do we see ourselves and our own contribution? Jesus said,

> Why do you see the speck in your neighbor's eye, but do not notice the log in your own eye? Or how can you say to your neighbor, 'Let me take the speck out of your eye,' while the log is in your own eye? You hypocrite, first take the log out of your own eye, then you will see clearly to take the speck out of your neighbor's eye. (Matt 7:3-5)

We need each other. From both the pulpit and the pew, we each need to take an intense look at ourselves and see what we can do to improve. For holy preaching that touches and reaches the world in which we live, we need spiritual formation and we need homiletical skill. The two work together.

To recap from earlier, a preacher continually grows in his ability to paint an icon by how he invests his life (formation), composes his words (content), and expresses them in the homily (delivery). *The Basic Plan for Ongoing Formation of Clergy* says it this way: "Integration is at the heart of ongoing formation, as priests grow in bringing together *who* they are and *what* they do. Their growth is really a growing integrity or connectedness of their ministry and their life."[40]

Similarly, listeners can grow by being spiritually formed as well as being trained in listening skills in order to be receptive to the message so that they encounter the living God through the Sunday homily. God gave the church both priestly and lay perspectives to keep a healthy balance. They are not opposed but complementary.

Through baptism, the layperson has "put on Christ" (Gal 3:27). Through holy orders, a deacon, priest, or bishop is "signed with a special character and are conformed to Christ the Priest in such a way that they can act in the person of Christ the Head."[41] Though on parallel tracks, we can link arms for the glory of God. Our goal is to preach the gospel of Jesus Christ: first to be renewed ourselves and then from there to bring love and joy to the world in which we live.

6

The World of the Listener

[Lord,] I believe; help my unbelief! (Mark 9:24)

A Plea for Good Preaching

Laypeople *want* to talk about preaching. Starting in 1975, Bishop Ken Untener of the Saginaw, Michigan, diocese kept a notebook in his pocket and questioned laypeople every chance that he could—when meeting strangers, at parties, on airplanes: "I bought a pocket notebook and began to ask people (Colombo-style) what they liked and didn't like about homilies. I asked only 'the people in the pew,' that is . . . (those who) had no particular axe to grind. . . . They talked; I wrote. Surprising how willing people were (and are) to talk about this. Others who overheard chimed in."[1]

Deacon David Shea also found a deep passion to talk about preaching in his listener study in his Cincinnati archdiocese. He wrote, "[I]t is unambiguous that Catholics—both adults and teens alike—care deeply about the Sunday homily."[2] In my own consulting work, a parish catechetical leader was busy recruiting youth at "doughnut Sunday" for preaching preparation teams for phase one of the CONNECT process; the adults sitting next to the youth at the tables chimed in to beg, "Can we help too?"[3]

People want to talk. From the first chapter, the "how's the preaching?" conversation already occurs at dinner tables and in parking lots and in the car on the way home from Mass. The folks in the pew have seen that preaching can make a positive impact, as it did for the freshman boy who got over his nightmares as a result of his deacon's homilies. They also see friends and family walk away because of the preaching. They hear more homilies than their homilists ever do. From the last chapter, the Perception Gap is palpable on the pew side of the disparity: though it may not seem so important to those who preach, to those who listen, it is vital. Preaching makes a difference. The hope of the laity is high, higher than most preachers realize.[4]

Fervor for "Father"

Laypeople's expectations for the personal holiness of clergy are also high. Priests and bishops and deacons carry much authority in the minds of Mass-attending Catholics, especially when compared to other leaders in everyday life. From the data in chapter 2, five of the six people who attend Mass regularly are not involved in other parish activities. So they know the homilists by name; they do not know them personally. They operate out of their own mental image of what a "priest" or "deacon" is supposed to be.

On page three of my survey, one sixteen-year-old boy, Tony, was asked to evaluate the preacher whom he last heard. He circled that he strongly agreed that his preacher was friendly to him, treated him with respect, and called him by name. Was the priest approachable? Did he interact with young people regularly? Was he real and in touch with the world? Well, sort of. When Tony got to the descriptor, "exudes a love for Jesus," he circled, "Strongly agree." Then he penned in a remark to the author of the survey: "Yeah, he's a priest?" as if to say, "duh, lady, of course. . . ." His priest was *expected* to exude a love for Jesus. How could it be otherwise?

THE PERSON OF THE PREACHER		
Please circle the number that gives your most accurate response.	Strongly Agree (1)	Somewhat Agree (2)
13. This preacher is friendly to me.	(1)	2
14. This preacher treats me with respect.	(1)	2
15. This preacher calls me by name.	(1)	2
16. This preacher interacts with young people regularly.	1	2
17. This preacher is approachable, easy to talk to.	1	2
18. This preacher exudes a love for Jesus. *Yeah, he's a priest?*	(1)	2

Exudes a love for Jesus? "Yeah, he's a priest?"

One reason that the abuse scandals have hit so hard is that laypeople expect profound holiness from their clergy—it should "come with the job." The failings of clergy stick in the public memory because they are so unexpected. Pressures in this highly visible role can come from this (sometimes over-) exaltation that clergy receive from the laity. I recently heard a bishop at lunch shake his hands and plead, "I'm only human!"

High opportunity comes with that high hope. Because of that intrinsic authority, even a small improvement to preach more effectively will make a sizable difference. A preacher who connects his message to the needs and longings of his people can fire them up to impact the world in which they live.

The World of the Laity

Laypeople live in a lovely world. Laypeople live in a challenging world. We have pockets of fervor. We have pockets of ambivalence. Is God at work in the temporal world? Certainly. Is the face of God obscured by the temporal world? Certainly.[5] To live a Christian life as a layperson is to live within a paradox; we live in a world of belief which is also a world of unbelief.

To cast lay life as a battle between the churchy "us in here" versus the secular "them out there" is to diminish the lay calling. The vision laid out by the documents of the Second Vatican Council paints a life of beauty: the role of the laity is to name the joys and the pains and the struggles of everyday life and to transform them to the glory of God: "Christ's redemptive work . . . includes also the renewal of the whole temporal order. Hence the mission of the Church is not only to bring the message and grace of Christ to men and women but also to penetrate and perfect the temporal order with the spirit of the Gospel. In fulfilling this mission of the Church, the Christian laity exercises their apostolate both in the Church and in the world, in both the spiritual and the temporal orders."[6]

> In a world full of words, whose words will be heard?

The challenge and the opportunity of Sunday preaching is to empower the laity to transform that culture. But in a world full of words, whose words will be heard?

Words and More Words

In his homily for the Sunday vigil Mass at World Youth Day 2011, Pope Benedict XVI spoke 1,384 words as he addressed young people in seven languages.[7] A conversational Catholic homily contains about 1,000 to 1,200 words. An average Protestant sermon uses 1,400 to 1,800 words. Historically, orations of old were longer: in 1747, John Wesley's sermon, "Almost Christian," wound through 3,458 words and was the important word-event of his day.[8] In our day, where do those thousand-word Sunday homilies fit?

An iPod classic in the pocket of an American teenager can contain up to 1,200,000 words.[9] The average American household receives 848 pieces of junk mail per year.[10] Approximately 130 billion spam emails are sent every day.[11] We live in an over-communicated society. We "tighten the intake valve." We are inundated by noise. We have become adept at tuning out that which does not affect us. This is a necessary act of self-preservation.

If laypeople live in a culture that is learning how not to listen, how does that affect the one thousand words of Sunday preaching?[12] The first question now asked is "Does this pertain to me?" If "yes," then we pay attention. If "no," whether young or old, we toss the junk mail, delete the spam, and turn off the brain. This mental habit also transfers to the homily.

In addition, a monologue from the pulpit is becoming a foreign medium. Communication is evolving into a two-way conversation, especially among the internet-accustomed young. We are becoming a visual society, not experienced with oral discourse. We are swayed as much by subjective impressions as by objective analysis—the purposeful mental scrutiny of a spoken message is becoming rare. Students now take notes from a visual presentation on a screen (as in a PowerPoint) rather than having to translate from the words in the ear to a pen on the paper (as in a lecture).

So what words will effectively get the gospel message into a listener's brain? To understand that question, we have to ask, "What is already in the minds of our people as they pass through our church doors?"

Churchy Words Gone Flat

In chapter 2, we looked at what the Heath brothers call, "The Curse of Knowledge"—the tune that is playing in my head is not playing in yours.[13] We see this consistently at Mass. We stand as the priest recites the eucharistic prayer. He uses the "churchy" words of sacrifice, grace, salvation, mercy, incarnate, redemption, and so on.

These prayers rely on a memory of stories and images from sources that we as the community have in common, a give-and-take of shared language and human experience. Yet these words and stories are no longer in the common memory. Cultural changes have rendered them almost meaningless.

For example, since child-raising practices changed in the 1960s, where there is no punishment, there is no need for mercy: the tremble from "You are in trouble!" may be in the childhood experience of older adults in the pew and in the background of an older preacher, but many younger people have never had that experience. So who needs mercy?

If there is no such thing as sin, if there is no possibility of hell, who needs salvation? From what do we need to be saved? And what does it mean to need a Savior if there is nothing to be saved from? If the image of God has shrunk to "my buddy" or "my butler" and no bigger than I am,[14] but he is more demanding and not very "nice," then why would I want to follow or believe in Him/Her/It?[15]

We cannot presume that theological concepts are understood by those who listen to them used in a homily. "Churchy words" have gone flat. Unless we pump air into theological language, many listeners do not have the knowledge or the underlying experience to fill in those meanings.

> "Churchy words" have gone flat. Unless we pump air into theological language, many listeners do not have the knowledge or the underlying experience to fill in those meanings.

What difference does that make? Researchers have found that comprehension (and not entertainment) is what maintains a listener's attention.[16] Comprehension may be assumed by the preacher, but after a homily, there is no test, no objective measure of listener understanding. So preachers are left in a quandary: "What are my people 'getting' from my preaching?" and "How much of my intended message actually gets into their hearts and minds" and "Does it change the way that they live their lives?" When the feedback loop is broken, preachers are left to wonder.

Sources of "Boring"

More than fifty percent (52.4 percent) of all of the students who responded to my thesis study said that the preaching that they had heard in the past year was "flat and boring." About one of three of the preachers evaluated had delivery difficulties, described by students with such words as rambling, monotony, repetition, couldn't understand their English, or lack of a main point. Those "difficulties" are fairly obvious sources of boring.

Neurologists and psychologists have begun to study boredom more intensely. They hypothesize that boredom is related to a failure in the neural pathways that control the ability to pay attention.[17] Paying attention has been found to be closely correlated with understanding.[18] Even preachers with first-rate delivery skills routinely use "churchy words," and as a result, their well-crafted preaching is described as "lofty." It goes right over the heads of their listeners, especially those who are younger, less educated, and whose first language is not English. The listeners stop paying attention. Eucharistic prayers become just "words."[19] The preaching is mentally categorized as "something the priest says" or "church talk." If not translated into the everyday life of the person in the pew, then the two cultures run in parallel without really communicating. The preacher assumes the listener understands. The listener tunes out. Nobody says anything in the Loud Silence. The words continue. The message does not connect. The cycle goes round and round. How frustrating is that?

The challenge in Sunday preaching is that there is so much noise vying for our peoples' attention. The opportunity for the field of homiletics is that there is so much research available about attention. What does it mean for a listener to pay attention? What goes on within a listener's mind while a preacher is speaking?

Paying Attention

First, attention is selective.[20] People are most alert to things that are new, unique, or novel.[21] A mission preacher, for example, is a fresh voice in a parish. He can say the same things that the homilist says every Sunday, but he is heard (at least at first). When a parishioner couple travels for the winter, they pay close attention to new experiences, thoughts, and ideas and thus bring back the bulletin from the "great" parish in _____. Mission trips, retreats, service projects, and conferences also have a high level of impact for this same reason. To get folks (of any age) out of their comfort zone helps them to pay attention.

What people have seen before becomes part of the scenery.[22] The mind grows used to processing familiar sounds, sights, smells, and experiences. Religious rituals can fade into the background, and as a result, they weave a web of experience at the edge of our focus; *something* is processed without conscious attentiveness of that processing.[23] This becomes part of the fabric of life; a rich fabric, but perhaps not one that stands front and center in the mind (like mom's oatmeal compared to Thanksgiving dinner, from chapter 5).

Attention is also hierarchical: we attend most to what matters most.[24] What matters most? That which is "similar to 'me'": children watch older children; teenagers attend to other teenagers for clues to a social situation;

and clergy present diocesan convocations because the ordained respond well to the ordained.[25] When people are time-pressed or feel mentally overwhelmed, they also pay more attention to negative impressions. To gain attention, a speaker can hook into a topic or illustration that matters most on that particular day.

Though multitasking has been touted as *the* modern way of processing, studies show that it does not work. It wastes more time than it saves. It may also kill our concentration and creativity.[26] Attention is limited. We can only truly pay attention to many things if their processing is routine or doesn't take much effort.[27] Driving a car while drinking coffee, adjusting the radio, and talking on a speaker phone only works when driving is an "over-learned" skill. (A new driver may rear-end the car in front of her when trying to do all of that.)

Attention tends to wander when the mind is given free space or nothing on which to focus. The focusing of attention can also be trained, especially if the listener is invested in the person or the message.[28] Fr. [D], who described his practice of wandering the church before Mass in the opening to the last chapter, relied on that development of friendship to give him an edge in getting his peoples' concentration: "They pay attention to their friend."

The engagement of listeners depends on capturing and then maintaining their attention. Untener describes one form of nonverbal feedback as "The Fidget Level." He maintains that, "Homilies generally start out with zero fidget level. A good homily will retain this from beginning to end. . . . If the fidget level starts to rise . . . we can be sure there is a homily problem—too long, too abstract, too many thoughts, not connected with life, no depth, and so on."[29] One eighteen-year-old, Leah was passionate about God and her faith. Nevertheless, when asked to describe the preaching at her parish, she described her restlessness from the homily that she last heard:

> Confusing! [The preacher] seems like he is wandering through
> the jungle, hacking away with a machete with *no* idea of where

---

Factors of attention:

Novel, unexpected—the mind is sharp.

The same-old-same-old—it fades into the background.

Attention is limited—multitasking does not work.

Distraction is everywhere—internal and external.

Attention can be trained.

he is going. He has no idea of what he is going to say when he gets up there and makes it up, wanders around as though, "well . . . there's something we haven't heard yet . . . so . . . let's throw that in. . . ." He knows the jungle, probably better than all of us, but he doesn't know where he is going in it. If he would make a path, I could follow him.

Interviewer: How are you doing with following him?

It depends on how much I'm trying to follow. . . . I usually . . . try to hang in there for about two minutes; I'm *always* hopeful . . . and if it's not going anywhere, it feels like it just goes into my head and trickles down to my feet.

Distractions come from all directions; attention can be divided.[30] Internal distractions, like Leah's, can come from the homily itself: she cannot follow what the preacher is saying, thus the mental energy of trying to follow a message with "*no* idea where [it] is going" muddles her mind until she just gives up: "It just goes into my head and trickles down to my feet." A homily can distract itself: a disturbing story or disrespectful comment can make listeners mentally stop, especially when it is unexpected—they hear nothing more of what is said because their mental resources are still processing the thought that captured them.

Diversions from the message can also come from internal conflicts: for instance, researchers have found that a third of the people who are in their mid-50s and up (many of our listeners) have some sort of ongoing neck or back pain. What does that do to the ability to pay attention to a long homily?[31] A family feud in the car can simmer in a father's mind well past the Gospel and the homily, sometimes to be resolved through the sign of peace. The pending death of a pet, the girl sitting two pews ahead (Does she like me? Should I ask her out?), or the outcome of yesterday's football game or band competition may be the focus of a youth's mind during the annual parish budget report. Each person sitting in the pew has a head full of thoughts which can divert his or her attention from the intended homiletical message. Then add in the external factors: the crying of a child, people walking to the bathroom, a middle-aged man texting on his smartphone, the usher counting heads, a toddler jumping up and down, the piece of gum under the pew, a hearing aid with a high-pitched whine, a dog wandering into Mass . . . and welcome to Catholic pew-sitting life.

When expectations for the homily are low, attentiveness is also low. In the same focus group as Leah, seventeen-year-old Leo is sprawled on the couch with his long legs stretched onto the ottoman. When asked to describe his response to Leah's "machete-hacking" homilist, he laughs:

> I zone out within, like . . . once he stands up to walk to the pulpit.
>   In one ear and out the other . . .
>
> Interviewer: Is that based on your previous experience?
>
> Yup. In one ear and out the other.
>
> Interviewer: Why do you come?
>
> You come because your parents say, "Get in the car."

Why Do You Come to Mass?

Leo is not unusual. When queried, "Why did you go to Mass this Sunday?" almost one out of three (32 percent) of those youth who were regularly attending Mass checked, "Because I was required to." Parents struggle to get their kids to church (and it can be a struggle) and then they hope and pray for a homiletic message that will inspire their child. When I have spoken about my search to connect our Sunday preaching with our youth, those who have responded most passionately have been parents (and grandparents). They ache for the homily to connect with their kids.

Common wisdom would suggest that those who were "required to be there" would rate the homily more poorly than those who responded that they came to Mass "to worship God" (41.3 percent). This was not the case. Though their responses to the homily were somewhat lower, there was no statistically significant difference between the reasons for coming to Mass and the perception of the homily. Just because mom or dad said, "Get in the car" did not mean that their kids evaluated the homily differently (negatively *or* positively) than those who went willingly. This is good news for parents: making kids go to Mass does not hurt their response to the homily—it rises and sinks on its own merits.

This is tough news for homilists: it is often assumed that those who sit in the pews are believers. That assumption is not necessarily accurate. When the young people in my study characterized their own spiritual lives, of ten factors, "trying to be a good person" was the highest value. After that came: getting good grades; getting along with my parents; having an active social life, and so on. Second to last was "putting God first in my life." Dead last? "Prayer."[32] One priest described his awareness of this range of belief: "When I'm preaching, I'm preaching for the guy who brought his girlfriend who hates Catholics, or for the girl who has

---

Tough questions for tough times

(For personal evaluation for a pew-sitter)

1. On a scale of one to ten, how much do you prepare for Sunday Mass? In prayer? By reading the Scriptures? By fasting for an hour? By dressing for the occasion? By getting family members there? By setting aside distractions?

2. What is on your mind as you slide into the pew at Mass? How long does it take for you to get focused on the Mystery who is God?

3. When you are listening to a homily, what are you listening for? Look at factors of your own receptivity: What attitude do you bring to that homily? Does your receptivity depend on who is preaching? What hard feelings might you need to overcome to hear God speaking in the homiletical message? At what point do you stop listening? What captures your attention?

4. When you walk out of Mass, how did your encounter with God (or lack thereof) change the way that you behave in the rest of your life?

5. When your friends, family, colleagues think of people of deep faith and holiness, are you likely to be among the top ten that come to their minds?

6. What image of faith springs up when your people hear your name? Are you known mostly for something else? Where do you find your identity, and how does that relate to God?

7. Do you have a reputation for treating people with caring, kindness, and love? What memories of "Christian" and "Catholic" do you give to folks in the "non-churchy" world?

---

her husband with her who doesn't want any part of this—now *that* is the person that I am preaching to."

It may seem to the preacher that the homily floats out into a vacuum. It does not. The voices of the outside world run full tilt inside the minds of the listeners as they walk in the door. A thousand memories sit down each Sunday in our pews.[33] The homily can tie into those thoughts or it can ignore that they are there.

Seminary training that has traditionally surrounded the homily has taught the aspiring preacher to ask

> A thousand memories sit down in our pews each Sunday.

himself, "What do I want to say?" and/or with *lectio divina*, "What does God want to say?" This then moves to, "How do I craft a homily that has one main point, supporting illustrations, (maybe a joke?) and some application to take home?"[34] Homiletical evaluations reinforce these elements as goals for the homily.[35] This launches from an implicitly sender-side starting point and ends with "Here is my homily. I hope you like it."

If we are looking for the homily to bring the listener into an encounter with God, the effort to craft a beautiful message is a waste of time and energy if it does not connect with the listener. For the seminarian in chapter 2, when the message went over his head all the way through high school, it was two or three hours of the homilist's time squandered and eight minutes of wasted opportunity for the young listener, each week, times fifty-two weeks in a year.[36] Busy homilists do not have that kind of time and energy to waste.

Motivation and the Energy to Listen

From the body language that they see on Sunday, presiders (and altar servers) sometimes question, "Are they listening?" The backward lean, the crossing of the arms, and the closing of the eyes are often postures that indicate that someone has pulled out and is disengaged with the message.[37] I asked a professor to tell me how Sunday preaching can connect with unmotivated listeners. He replied that there are no unmotivated people—all people are motivated by something; the key is to find out what motivates them.[38] That shift of mindset can spur parents, teachers, coaches, and preachers to ask: What gets this kid out of bed in the morning to go to school? What motivates a man or woman to drive I-95 through rush hour to get to work? What prompts an athlete to run a 146-mile race from Death Valley to California's Mount Whitney? Each person is motivated by what he or she values.

> There are no unmotivated people. All people are motivated by something. The key is to find out what motivates them and hook into that. Then stretch.

What is the key to motivation? Find out what fuels the fervor. When we are driven, we grow enthusiastic about doing the things that help us to get where we want to go. In a high energy state, listeners will pay careful attention. For example, in the messages of Blessed John Paul II, young people found the image of the "adventure" of the gospel to be highly motivating. He gave them a slight touch of risk and a vision that they were an essential part of a team to better the world. How motivating is that?

Hearers who are not motivated to listen to a homiletical string of words will not apply effort toward processing it. As Leo in the focus group said, it goes "in one ear and out the other." The passionate Leah and the indifferent Leo may sit together in the same pew, eat the same doughnuts at breakfast, and ride in the same car to Mass. Who knows what runs in their heads?

Motivation to listen is influenced by personal relevance:[39] Does this communication pertain to me? Does it speak to my life issues? Does it matter to how I define myself? Does it have a direct bearing on what I do today? Messages that motivate are: (1) consistent with the listener's values, goals and needs; and (2) a little bit risky and somewhat inconsistent with that listener's prior attitudes."[40] In short, to motivate: tie in and then stretch. How does that relate to Sunday preaching?

Preaching the Paschal Mystery

This takes us straight to the Paschal Mystery. The paradoxical world in which people live is full of life, death, and resurrection. You and I believe and yet, we don't believe. The two elements of motivation—tie in and stretch—parallel the message of the church: first, acknowledge the lives that people lead (tie in), and then, second, name the grace of the gospel that moves the faithful closer to God (stretch).

Catholic preaching is weak when it focuses on one element to the exclusion of the other. Listeners may enjoy a homily that relates to them and to their lives. If it doesn't stretch them to become more like Jesus, it may have been a pleasant interlude, but ultimately it leaves them flat. It does not motivate. Alternatively, a homily that tries to stretches with the gospel without tying into everyday life is like a rubber band that has no hook on which to anchor the pull. That means "this does not concern me" which turns into "tune it out."

The role of the homily is to gather together all of those grains of thought and experience from the people in the pew and then elevate them to God. Then, like the eucharistic action, bring the Word of God to the people to feed them. We become what we eat at the table of the Word which then leads us to the table of the Lord. This is what Jesus did. He spoke and acted in concrete ways, pulling people together and then stretching them toward divinization, to become more like God.

This simple way of relating applies to preaching, teaching, and evangelization: to help people to grow, tie in, and then stretch. Fr [T] described it this way in his interview: "The Paschal Mystery never gets old. . . . So when you're able as a preacher . . . to name the woundedness, the pain, the hurt, the brokenness, whether it is the family relationships or society, however that is, then people are saying, alright I've been there too, I've been hurt, I'm lonely, heartbroken [tie in], then Christ is going to come in and heal that . . . [stretch]. It's all part of the Paschal Mystery, dying and rising . . . and that the only way you live is by dying . . . and it's great! So again, that never gets old."

In promoting the homily as an encounter with God, *Preaching the Mystery of Faith* says, "Ultimately the Lord's Paschal Mystery becomes the basis of all preaching. . . . This defines the preacher's task: enabling the whole community and each individual believer to draw on the power of the Holy Spirit and to say with one's whole being, 'Jesus is Lord,' and to cry out to God, 'Abba, Father!'"[41]

Go Deeper

"Go deeper" was a consistent plea from the young listeners in my doctoral study. "Deeper" does not mean to preach a more strident stance against the moral deficiencies of the world. It means to speak to the joys and pains of everyday life. It means to name the graces of how and where God is present. It means to tell the Good News of Jesus Christ. It means to lift the faithful with the gospel message to be better, to be stronger, to be more loving, to be more forgiving—in short, to grow in their abilities to handle the messiness of life in the strength of the Holy Spirit.

Who better to help a preacher to identify concrete needs than parishioners themselves? People in the pew may not be trained in scriptural scholarship. They may not have a formal theological education. They do know life. Rather than garnering abstractions about the culture "out there" by watching the news or reading the paper or checking an online blog, check the "local news" right in front of you: A grandfather can name the sense of God's love at seeing the tiny fingernails of his new premature grandson. A teenager can name the stomach-aching despair of losing a friend to suicide. A catechist can describe the glassy-eyed stare of an orphaned sixth grader when she speaks of a relationship with "God the Father." Those who live and breathe what is "out there" can help to concretize and localize our preaching. Connecting with the world in which we live and then stretching with the Good News—that is the heart of the new evangelization.

To connect with listeners, then, homily preparation begins, not with "What do I want to say?" but ties in with "What will they give me?" which then moves to gently stretch them with "What does Christ call them to?" To ask, "What are my peoples' struggles and needs?" leads to "Where is God already at work in their lives?" and then "How can I tie into that and then bring the gospel message to them in words that they understand?" In order to fulfill that mission, a homilist has to understand the concrete world of his own flock. That begins with listening to the listeners.

We have looked at the complexities that surround the Sunday homily through the eyes of history, clergy, and listeners. We now turn to look at the relationship between the pulpit and the pew. High school youth have much to say about the current state of the connections in Catholic preaching. They hanker to be heard.

Implications for Preachers

Homily preparation begins, not with "What do I want to say?" but:

"What will they give me?" → which then moves to gently stretch with → "What does Christ call them to?"

"What are my peoples' struggles and needs?" leads to → "Where is God already at work in their lives?" and then → "How can I tie into that and then bring the gospel message to them in words that they understand?"

In order to fulfill that mission, a homilist has to understand the concrete world of his own flock.

Connecting with Sunday Preaching and the Sunday Preacher

Let love be genuine; hate what is evil, hold fast to what is good; love one another with mutual affection. . . Do not lag in zeal, be ardent in spirit, serve the Lord. (Romans 12:9–11)

We were halfway through the discussion in one of the focus groups when a blond sixteen-year-old shifted his chair around the table to face me. He leaned forward and earnestly told the group that he planned to become a priest.[1] This discussion on how to connect young people and preaching interested him greatly. He passionately declared: "You need to get this information to the younger priests. This input could help the ones who are learning how to preach. Go to a seminary. Tell them what we have said."

Tell Them What We Have Said

What did they say? The final question in my survey offered the kids a chance to say anything at all to their homilist. Some simply expressed gratitude:

- "I would tell him how much his preachings help me in my life and how much I love going to Mass to hear him speak. He connects so well with others and keeps everyone interested."
- "Keep up the good work. I am always listening."
- "Thank you, Father, for how you guide me to be more faith-filled. I like how you are comforting and always there to help. I can't thank you enough."

Like the fire burning in the hearts of the disciples on their way to Emmaus, the encounter of preaching can have a long-term impact. A high school junior wrote how preaching has influenced him: "A lot of it had to do with accepting difficulties in life. Often, people will either turn to or turn away from God during the extremes in their life; the homilies I've heard usually kept me closer to God in these times." Through the opportunity of liturgical preaching, young people can thrive.

How common is this flourishing? What is the long-term "take-away" from Catholic preaching from this sample of 561 Catholic high school students?

The Long-term Effect of Preaching

One of the eighty-six questions in the survey asked the young people for their overall impression of the Sunday preaching that they had heard in the past year. From a bank of sixteen attributes, they could mark as many as characterized their experience of Catholic preaching.

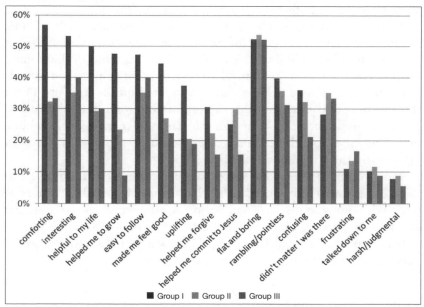

Table 7a

This question was repeated in the second half of the survey for those who attended Mass sporadically or only at their Catholic school; the chart illustrates all three group responses.[2] For those attending Mass, the homily traits selected by more than 50 percent of Group I respondents were these three: comforting; interesting; and flat, boring delivery. The lowest three responses were: frustrating; talked down to me; and harsh and judgmental.[3] The variations between the three groups were most striking in the positive take-away from the preaching—those who were not attending Mass (Groups II and III) did not find the homilies so uplifting, comforting, or helpful to faith growth. As noted in chapter 2, they were working out of a much more negative memory of preaching than those who consistently still listened to it.[4]

One of three youth who regularly attended Mass felt that it did not seem to matter that they were there. This was a constant written comment—the Sunday homily was targeted at the "older folks." As we saw earlier in the documents of the church, preaching as a source of faith growth in young people is a blind spot for the institutional church. Yet even though some feel marginalized,[5] around 50 percent checked that the preaching had been "helpful to my life" and "helped me grow in faith." Almost 40 percent could say that sometime in the past year, it had been "uplifting."

What about the negative attributes? Four of ten marked "rambling, pointless" as a characteristic of the homilies that they had heard in the last year. (In the next table [6b], there was a similar response to the homily "had a central idea," in question 27.) The kids often commented in their open-ended responses that preaching wandered off on tangents. These three sources of data suggest that digression from (or a lack of) a central point is a consistent attribute in almost half of the experiences of Catholic preaching. Shea found the similar responses to problems with clarity in his study in the Cincinnati archdiocese.[6]

Most young people characterized the preaching as both positive and negative. Intuitively it would seem that those who marked "interesting" and those who marked "flat, boring" would represent two different groups—the interested and the bored. Yet 98 percent of those who checked "interesting" also marked "flat, boring." The overall "take-away" is that the experience of Catholic preaching is a very mixed bag.

Evaluating the One Homily

Sunday preaching is a source for jokes, laments, and conversations. A seventeen-year-old retreat leader narrated the tale of her family dinner table discussion about her upcoming participation in one of the study's focus groups:

> I told my family about this [focus group], because they're like, "What's up? What's up with you, what are you doing tomorrow?"

(I've got a huge family.) And I was telling them, "Oh yeah, before [retreat meeting], I have this huge survey on, like, Catholic preaching," and then all my little brothers, they were just like, "Oh, my gosh, homilies. . ." (her voice dropped, deprecatingly in imitation) and my older brother was, like, "Yeah, homilies are awful" and we just started talking. . .

Anecdotes abound. Studies do not. Yet creating a really good homily is tough, and most homilists work hard at their preaching.[7] As seen in chapter 2, anecdotal evidence arises from memory. Memory of negative experience lingers longer and forms stronger emotions than positive recall, so how many well-crafted homilies does it take to balance out one unforgettably abysmal one? Can Catholic preaching be *that* bad? In this detective hunt for connection, I had to find that out.

Short-term Response

As the kids sat in their theology classes, all of them took the survey.[8] The first bank of questions about the preaching asked those attending Mass to evaluate the homily that they most recently heard; thus they did not get to pick who they evaluated. Two hundred and two distinct preachers were evaluated from six regions of the country, some more than once. From this cluster sample, one of the results that I shared in chapter 2 was that more than fifteen percent (15.6 percent) of the Mass-attending (Group I) high school youth surveyed *would* recommend that Sunday homily to a friend. Almost 40 percent said "No," they would not recommend it. The rest were ambivalent. If we were selling basketball shoes to a basketball team (those actively participating in that sport), that would be an unacceptably low "customer satisfaction" level. So how does that response break down into individual components?

The responses to ten questions[9] (#26–35) about the homily are listed in table 7b. Eighty-four percent (84 percent) of the respondents agreed that the homily talked about God and/or Jesus. (The other 16 percent were not sure or said that it did not.) Three of four felt that it spoke in words and images that they knew. The level of agreement dropped from there, and hesitancy began to set in for the other eight homiletical characteristics. Sixty-one percent (61 percent) agreed that the homily was sincere and personal; almost 30 percent did not agree or disagree.

"Sort of" characterizes their responses to "opened me to better receive the Eucharist," "helped me in the struggles of life," and "made me feel

Table 7b

	Talked about following God, Jesus (29)	Used words, images, or examples I know (28)	Was sincere and personal (32)	Helped me to understand the Bible (33)	Full of conviction (31)	Had a central idea (27)	Opened me to better receive the Eucharist (34)	Helped me in the struggles of daily life (30)	Inspired discussion with family, friends	Made me feel full of life
Strongly Agree	50.9	34.7	27.1	22.0	17.2	16.4	13.4	12.7	8.1	7.5
Somewhat Agree	33.1	38.5	33.7	30.9	22.1	30.4	30.8	22.7	15.8	38.4
Neither Agree nor Disagree	12.5	17.5	29.9	32.0	46.3	24.6	39.0	37.1	28.5	37.7
Somewhat Disagree	3.2	6.9	7.9	12.0	9.8	17.1	10.6	18.6	20.1	12.7
Strongly Disagree	0.4	2.4	1.4	3.1	4.6	11.6	6.2	8.9	27.5	3.8

Source: *Are You Talking to Me?*, qq. 26–35

full of life." "Had a central idea that I can still remember" likewise had a mixed response.

That lack of remembering may have contributed to the reply that garnered the strongest disagreement: "inspired discussion with family and friends." The kid and their families did not talk about the homily after Mass. Unlike the lay leaders' description in chapter 2, most homilies were not particularly memorable; the message did not spread like wildfire throughout the city or over the internet; its "stickiness" was weak.

The Skills of Preaching to Connect

Young people pleaded for homiletical competence. In their open-ended responses to question about connection, they described what would connect for them. Homily content and delivery headed the list.

How to Connect in Content and Delivery

Homily Content	Work on Your Delivery Skills
• Come to our level, relate to my life	• Use good eye contact
• Bring meaning, be interesting	• Keep it relaxed
• Have emotional appeal	• Make it to the point
• Be personal and open with your life	• Speak clearly
• Help us—know our problems and speak to them	• Use words that people understand
	• Be organized
• Help us to understand/teach me	• Be enthusiastic
• Apply the gospel to my life	• Do not repeat yourself

Table 7c

What to Talk About

As we saw in the definition of motivation in the last chapter, pages and pages and pages of comments described how the homily has to hook into everyday life in order to connect:

- "For a preacher to connect with me, he must be able to see in the eyes of a kid/teenager. My deacon is very good at communicating with kids as much as he does with adults."

- "For a preacher to 'connect' with you, he needs to understand how I am as a person. He needs to be accustomed to what kids my age are going through."

- "The preacher needs to speak to me, not talk down to [me]. He or she also needs to put things in 'teenage terms' so I understand more fully."

Connect via a story that relates.

Motivation to listen is influenced by this personal relevance. Preachers are understandably leery about being "entertaining" in order to get kids' attention. The concerns about watering down the gospel are legitimate. But the young people did not ask for entertainment or for the gospel to be watered down. They asked for more depth, not less. They hoped for inspiration. They sought for the homily to be about a topic that touched their lives. When that happened, the connection felt tailored to them personally:

- "When a preacher connects with me, it means that he understands me and what I believe in. Also it means I understand him and feel as if his words mean something special to me."

- "They can apply gospel stories with real situations that I deal with in high school."

- "For a preacher to connect with me personally is when he describes an event that I can relate to, or if he is preaching about a topic that I find interesting."

Part of this relatability factor comes from the kids perceiving that the preacher knows what their world is like. Ries and Trout suggest, "You have to get off of your pedestal and put your ear to the ground. You have to get on the same wavelength. . . ."[10] When teenagers do not hear something that they relate to, they not only tune out to a particular message, but their way of positioning the preacher is colored. Since memories vary in salience, unfortunately negative perceptions most easily come to mind:

"For a preacher to connect with a young audience, he needs to be aware of current events in the news/media that pertain to their age group. When my priest rambles on and on about things I don't know/care about, I lose interest."

A variation of "relate to my life" was "let me relate to yours." There was much hope for a mutual flourishing and a concern for the welfare of the preacher as well. Both positively and negatively, the kids called for a "realness" that they gained through hearing the preacher's life experiences. This can be either implicit or explicit:

- "It made things clearer to me and I felt like that my priest really understood what I was dealing with. It was almost like he was talking directly to me."

- "They've been in my footsteps before. Been there before. Admits it's not always easy."

- "For a preacher to connect with me he must bring in real life situations and talk of his personal triumphs/failures."

- "If I feel the priest is being genuine about his experiences/emotions/thoughts and not making too many assumptions/talking down, I can relate as a fellow human with experiences/emotions/thoughts."

Students sought for content that was meaningful or interesting. They were not looking for fluff. Those who were attending Mass wanted substance. This came through both positively and negatively:

- "Preachers rarely connect with me because half the time they aren't saying anything interesting. Most homilies don't have any practical use to me because there's no real world application. Instead of telling me what the readings were, how about trying to describe why the readings actually matter in today's world? The only time preachers actually keep me interested is if they tell a relevant story, or describe an overlying theme of the readings instead of reiterating them."

- "To 'connect' with a preacher for me means that the preacher interests me, holds my attention, and makes me understand God more. I want to feel inspired by God's love and the stories I hear. Nowadays, it is hard to connect with all the hate in the world. . ."

Two boys raved about the intellectual quality of their preachers' homilies at school:

- "They were smart and shared relatable and intellectual ideas in their homilies. They were enthusiastic about what they were talking about, not bored. They had a way with words, well-spoken and gave educated insight into their homilies."
- "I also like the [religious order] homilies I hear at school Masses. They seem to challenge me more intellectually as opposed to just hearing the same about trying to be better and don't sin!"

Many more sought for intellectual understanding:

- "When a preacher connects with me, it means that he or she has spoken truthful words of God with me. . . . I feel as if God is sitting in front of me and I can understand Him. Also the role God plays in my life as well as what my responsibilities as a daughter of God are, should be highlighted in the preaching."
- "For a preacher to 'connect' with me would mean for him to understand the times we are in but still use his experiences and the word of God to teach the truth."

When a preacher is convinced about the message, he is also convincing:

- "When a preacher 'connects,' they are interested in who you are, and they want to convey an important message."
- "To be open and truthful. Show excitement, respect."

Similarly to connection in general, a large number of kids want to be understood and helped by the preaching that they hear. When a message applies to a young person's life, they are grateful. When it seems that the preacher understands their problems and can speak to them, the students are uplifted. When they learn to apply the gospel to their lives, they feel connected.

- "It was good to hear a great homily by my favorite priest, he makes the gospel into life lessons that we can incorporate into our lives."
- "For a preacher to connect with you, they must be able to see out of your eyes and to feel what you are feeling and truly understand where you come from."
- "When a preacher is speaking, his message should relate to my life and his life. I want to hear a personal story about him, and I want him to apply it to my life, as though he was only talking to me. That is a connection, for me at least."

When faith is fragile, the world is confusing. So much conflicting information comes their way. In an individual homily, one way to differentiate from all of the noise is to meet the personal need of the listener. In meeting the need, the homily should be as simple and clear as possible. Less is more. As teens grow, their view of the world broadens. They have many questions. The adult world does not always make sense to a child-becoming-adult. When preached simply, an image, story, or statement can "hook" into their mental framework. A profound analogy can further understanding. For a fifteen-year-old Latino boy, a visual image from a homily resonated with his life experience:

> It was a couple of month's ago and I think I was having an overall bad week (sports, grades, etc). His homily talked about perseverance, the "light at the end of the tunnel." I just remember feeling way better after that.

When the message is distilled to a core concept, that idea reminds the hearer of what is important.[11] Beliefs then change, which adjusts attitude and thus behavior.[12] A seventeen-year-old Ukrainian Catholic boy describes just such a change as the result of a homily:

> The homily helped me see a bird's-eye view of life or the "big picture." I started to stop worrying about the petty arguments about things that didn't really matter that were harming my relationship with my family (parents and siblings).

How to Talk About It

Preaching delivery also indicates a preacher's connection: use good eye contact, keep it relaxed, make it to the point, speak clearly, use words that people understand, be organized, be enthusiastic, do not repeat yourself. High school students who are involved in drama, speech, and debate are especially attentive to the delivery of public speaking. In giving his advice to preachers, one seventeen-year-old boy summarized the comments of his peers:

> Personal stories. How message of readings apply to "real world." Be a good story-teller. Talk loudly and slowly. Include pitch and tone into your talk (when applicable, no monotone). Call to action. Open with a semi-relevant joke. Be honest and sincere. Keep it fairly short: 1 to 3 examples will suffice (as opposed to 6 to 10).

The Relational Skills of a Preacher's Connection

Many young people did not describe their connection with their preacher as linked to the words from the pulpit. They described connection as the social qualities of: being friendly; easy-going, approachable, and comfortable; he says hello and greets you outside of Mass. These interpersonal "soft skills" go a long way in connecting a young person with their parish preacher:

- "Yes, [ ] always greets me and regularly checks up on me in a caring fashion. He is fun when hanging out with but also is a great example and teacher of God's word."

- "A preacher that connects with me makes one feel welcome. At the beginning of Mass my priest greets my family and welcomes us to the parish."

To connect means to make me feel welcome.

Many respondents wanted to be known personally. Not just a face in the crowd, their plea was "know my name," "learn something about me," and "treat me as a friend":

- "I go to a very big parish so just knowing my name and some stuff about me makes me feel very connected to him."

- "They call me by name and we just have a natural connection and they are very easy going and easy to talk to."

- "The preacher should know who you are, by name. He should also know a little bit of your personality so that he can relate to your life and make the homilies relevant."

A third category of soft skills revolved around counseling, helping with problems, and "being there for you." There are times in teenagers' lives when they are highly vulnerable. The Sunday homily does not preach into a vacuum: parents, friends, relatives, and clergy as authority figures, role models, and heroes can have a lasting impact and create turning points in life. In their vision of connectedness, the kids saw their parish priest as a

To connect means to know my name.

potential companion as they travel the confusing journey of life. (The sacrament of reconciliation can also create such an opportunity, for those youth who still go). In the harried world of Catholic parish busyness, this pastoral counseling aspect of clerical life may not be as accessible as it was in the past, yet a large number of young people had high hopes that it could be so:

• "He tries actively to talk and help you, bring you closer to God."

• "For a preacher to connect with me, it means that we can have normal conversations and that I feel comfortable going to him for help or to talk."

• "They understand you and can relate/help you w/problems and advice."

• "You can feel like you can tell the preacher any of your problems and trust him."

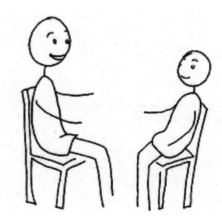

Connect by helping me with my problems.

What Kids Really Want to Say about How to Connect Outside of the Homily	
Relational Skill	**Youth Quote**
Be friendly and interested	"Say 'Hello: How are you doing; How is school,' etc.—the little things he should talk to young people about." "The preacher asks about my life, and is interested in my life, future plans, faith, and other aspects."
Show care and respect	"Let me know that I matter." "Don't treat me like I'm stupid." "Talk *down* less, and talk *to* more!"
Build trust	"'Connection' gives you this feeling that you have known them and developed a relationship with them over years. It also makes you feel . . . that you can trust that they will understand where you are coming from and you are safe with them."
Be approachable, comfortable	"It means a lot for a preacher to 'connect' with me, since I feel like I really belong to that community and they allow me to be comfortable like I'm at home."
Give the gift of presence	"For some, it means that they talk to you after and before church and they go to many activities or events in the parish."
Be other-centered	"A preacher connecting with me means he wants *me* to understand." "He has to know what its like for a teenager in 2013 and not in 1960."
Be a role model	"'Connecting' with a preacher makes me feel closer to God." "He . . . has a relationship with God that I want to model mine after."

Source: *Are You Talking to Me?*, qq. 24 and 63.

Table 7d

Pathways to Encounter

If an encounter with God is the purpose of Sunday preaching, how are we to determine when that happens? "Encounter" is an elusive term. How are we to know whether or not someone has "met" God? We believe in a God of revelation: there are moments when we "touch" or "see" or "experience" God, by grace in the working of the Holy Spirit. How do we objectively look at that?

In my survey, 55 percent of the high school students who attended Mass regularly could describe some experience of growing in faith through the preaching that they had heard in the past year.[13] Their responses indicate that there are clear fruits of effective preaching. One seventeen-year-old young lady described how the homily had revealed the face of God for her:

> I was really confused about what God wanted me to do when I walked into Mass. That week, the homily was all about giving your life up to God and trusting in Him. I have had other experiences like this where the homily is exactly what I needed to hear that week. It just helped me believe that God was real and was trying to talk to me.[14]

How do we identify the movement of the Holy Spirit? Are there identifiable fruits of the Connector? When these qualitative responses were categorized, they gave us some indications of what those might be.

Some young people described moments when they saw their faith more clearly. For them the invisible became more visible: "The homily motivated me to worship God more and opened my eyes to how I should worship God and respect other people."

Similar to their descriptions of "connection," a tone of energy, lightness, and joy characterized their comments. Though the extensive search of church documents did not mention the Sunday homily as a source of faith growth for young disciples, these students did. Of these, some said that the ongoing experience produced a positive emotional response within worship:

- "Listening to the homily just uplifts my heart and I just feel really good about myself when I hear about Jesus. . ."

- "Well, when you hear a good homily you fall into a state of calmness. It's hard to explain but it's peaceful and you feel like a different person in a way."

The largest category of response centered on a deepening of understanding, whether to better understand God or life, church teaching or Scripture, or one's vocation.[15] This richer awareness led to an epiphany marked by courage, comfort or inner leading:

- "The experience was like I actually know that God listens to me. He may not answer me right away or when I want, but he does hear me. He also forgives me when I do wrong and will help me through life as long as I follow and worship him to the best of my ability."

- "The Sunday homily taught me about Jesus and his teachings. Hearing and learning about the goodness in the world made me want to do as HE did."

Some described a change of heart or attitude as a result of the connection of the preaching:

- "Whatever worries I had, they would preach something relating to that that would calm me down."
- "Well, it made me feel like I should be thankful for everything I have."

A large number also spoke of an intensified spirituality or deeper relationship with God. Most of these responses used the word "closer" or "strengthened." This hunger expressed itself in both general and specific ways:

- "It helped me to understand God more and grow closer to him."
- "When I heard Fr. J preach, he touched me."
- "I felt a stronger longing for God. I wanted a better relationship with Him."

Finally, a common result of the homily was a modification in the teen's behavior: to help others, to be better, to go to church more, to imitate Jesus, and to forgive. Scripture calls it "go and do likewise." Here is how they express this conversion:

- "The experience was not really divine or euphoric but rather contemplative, forcing me to think about certain parts of my life that I could or should have changed."
- "That experience uplifted me because I felt as if I could change myself and strive with motivation to become a good, God loving person."
- "Fr. A gave a homily about LOVING HUMILITY. It helped me want to grow more deeply into my relationship with God. It made me want to be a better person."
- "[It] made me want to be more like Jesus."

Some young listeners put a lot of energy into processing a homiletic message. They will work to sort out ideas, they may be emotionally connected to the person of the preacher, have a strong commitment to God, and may have had positive experiences with homilies that have helped them. These high-energy listeners expect homilies to connect. Their comments express the transformative power of preaching in the ongoing experience of liturgy. If the task for the church is to transmit its message to the next generation, these responses indicate that it can certainly do so. God's Word goes forth into the world. This is cause for celebration. The kingdom of God is here.

Pathways to Encounter through the Homily		
	Positive Encounter: 55% of those attending Mass regularly were able to describe some growth in faith in the past year through a homily. What was that experience like?	**Negative/Nothing Experience:** 45% of those attending Mass regularly could not describe an experience of growth in faith in the past year as a result of a homily. What was it like to sit in the pew for a year and not grow in faith?
Belief (What is God like?)	Revealed the face of God through the message of the homily	Obscured or distorted the face of God through the homily
Emotion	Sense of energy, lightness, life, joy	Tone of dullness, heaviness, waste of time
Understanding	A deepened appropriation of the gospel, saw faith more clearly	Miscomprehension of the gospel message; negatively impacted the image of the Church
Memory/Internal Story	Desired a deeper relationship with God/the Church.	Didn't want to be there, felt unnecessary or marginalized
Behavior	Modified behavior to be a better person, changed attitude, wanted to be more like Jesus	Learned to ignore the homily; thought about walking away or going somewhere else

Source: *Are You Talking to Me?*, qq. 59, 60a, 60b

Table 7e

Long-term Homiletical Take-Away Can Also Obscure the Face of God

The kingdom of God is also not yet here. Some young people described spiritual growth as a result of homiletic take-away. Others told how homilies had not helped to strengthen their faith. Forty-five percent of those surveyed who regularly attend Mass could not recall an experience of preaching that had helped them to grow in their faith in the past year. These responses also coalesced into consistent themes. When asked to describe what that experience was like, they described symptoms of dullness, sleepiness, or heaviness. For some, the experience was emotionally painful:

- "It makes me frustrated and confused that the preaching doesn't help me grow in my faith. I hate not being able to focus my attention on the homily."
- "SAD."
- "It feels pointless."
- "If I am not helped in my faith when I come to Mass, at the moment I feel lost because I have nobody to help me understand God."

When the desire to grow is not met, it also has a cumulative dulling or demotivating effect for these young people who are still consistently going to church:

- "It feels like no one is really reaching out to me. I feel obligated to go to Mass."
- "I feel really dull during some homilies, and I feel myself counting down how much time I have until I can be done with it."

A second theme that reverberated throughout the comments of young people who were not growing in faith was "boring." If the message were coming through their cell phone, it was getting no signal. There was no connection. They described this weightiness as "watching it happen," the "same everything every time," and "not worth it." High school students described sources for "boring" as repetitiveness, lack of a central message, rambling, and poor delivery:[16]

- "The same point is made over and over and it gets boring. Sing a new song for once."
- "I usually end up spacing out during the homily and getting sleepy because of the rambling (which may have much meaning behind

it, but puts me to sleep). I end up losing concentration, thinking of other things or yawning."

A small number of young listeners dismissed the homily as unnecessary to their growth in faith. The expectation was that the homily was of no help. Not only was there no signal, the cell phone had been turned off as though there would be no service:

- "Honesty, I feel that I'm a pretty good person, so they don't do much."

- "Not having a preacher to connect with isn't life altering. I still have a family and friends I connect with. Most sermons come off as lectures and information shoved down your throat to me."

- "It depends when I go, some Sundays are brutally boring and others can hold my attention, it depends on the priest. I grow in faith through myself and my experiences, not a homily."

These listeners have shrunk inward and turned off the homily.

The ongoing fruit of disconnected preaching is that the encounter does not occur: the face of God is obscured or hidden; sometimes the face of God is misrepresented as unappealing or uncaring. Many in the pew (more than just youth) feel marginalized by a message that does not make an attempt to connect with them, as though they do not matter.

Seeking for Homiletic Excellence

How are we to evaluate ongoing homiletic excellence? As Harris said in chapter 1, the test of effective preaching is the fruit that it bears in its listeners.[17] The overarching symptoms of connection and faith growth give indications of how to evaluate how well we are doing:

1. Does the long-term experience of the homily encourage a healthy faith, spiritual energy, a sense of light, and the vibrancy to want to share the message? This imitates the connection of love in the Trinity.

2. Does the long-term experience of the preaching induce heaviness, plodding, dullness, and self-protective disconnectedness that block the movement of God and the flow of the Spirit?

As an eschatological event of the kingdom-of-God-is-here-but-not-yet-here, preaching is likely to contain elements of both. But if weighed on the balance, which fruit is the more evident—death or life? Weighed down or joyful? Despair or hope? Darkness or light? Flourishing or fading away?

Young people who continue to attend Mass through high school seem cautiously hopeful about preaching (see "Report Card from the Young Pew" in table 7f). If the event of preaching were a soccer game, most of them want to be out on the field and to be valued as a member of the team. They want to play. They are listening. McCarty, who has worked extensively with young people, describes his vision of their need in this way:

> There is no need to "water down" our theology or our teachings. Ministry with young people is not served by appeasing their youthfulness. Rather, the church must preach the authentic Jesus Christ, who challenged the world of his day and now the world of ours. They deserve the whole Gospel, the Gospel that calls young people to authentic discipleship. Young people are looking for a noble adventure, and the reign of God is that adventure.[18]

If asked the theological question of revelation, "God, are you still speaking?" many of these young folks would give a resounding "Yes!" If asked of their preacher, "Are you talking to me?" some would give a high five and state, "For sure." Others would say, "Um, well, . . . no, not really."

Young people are not seeking a faith that is blind and dark but a faith that is revealed and shining, challenging and motivating through the preaching that they hear. They hunger for both a human person and a personal message that will inspire them, give them direction, and be a vibrant living expression of what their faith life is to be.

The Reign of God Is a Noble Adventure

Young people ask for us to "go deeper." What does it mean to go deeper? Let us step aside for a moment from the world of data and analysis to enter into the realm of personal and communal memory. What is our experience of the God who calls? What (and Who) comprises this noble adventure? And how do those memories impact the way that we preach, share, and further the Story of Stories?

Report Card from the Young Pew

Age of Clergy Evaluated	Preachers Evaluated	Basis of Evaluation
(in # of student responses) 25–35 years old: 27 36–45 years old: 58 46–60 years old: 125 61–79 years old: 73 80+ years old: 7 No response: 4 **Total: 294 student evaluations**	184 Priests 8 Deacons 1 Bishop 9 No designation ――――――― **202 Clergy**	1. Students in the survey: 561 2. What to evaluate: the Sunday homily last heard 3. Who evaluated: Only those high school students who attended Mass at least once/month were included: 294 fit that criterion (52%) 4. Did not evaluate, responded to a different set of questions: Baptised Catholics who were not attending Mass at least once/month: 176 (31%); non-Catholics who attended Catholic schools: 91 (16%)

Subject	Response				
Person of the Preacher *(% that strongly agree or somewhat agree)*	Treats me with respect: 92.8%	Exudes a love for Jesus: 92.6%	Friendly to me: 91.0%	A role model for me: 81.6%	Calls me by name: 56.6%
Quality of the Homily *(% that strongly agree or somewhat agree)*	Talked about following God/Jesus: 84%	Had a central idea: 46.8%	Full of conviction: 39.3%	Made me feel full of life: 45.9%	Inspired discussion among family and friends: 23.9%
Age/ Person of the Preacher Correlations	No overall statistical correlation found between age of preacher and the averaged ten qualities of the "person of the preacher." Young and old clergy were equally highly regarded.				
Age/Homily Quality Correlations	No overall statistical correlation found between age of preacher and the averaged ten qualities of the homily.		Except: In the quality, "Unpacks the scriptures," younger preachers rated higher in a statistically significant way.		
Student grown in faith through the homily?	Could describe an experience of growth in faith through the homily in the past year: 55%		Could *not* describe an experience of growth in faith through the homily in the past year: 45%		
Why did you come to Mass?	To worship God: 41.3%	I was required to: 32.0%	To be with family and friends: 17.9%	To be entertained: 0.6%	Other: 4.7%	No response: 3.4%
Would you recommend this homily to a friend?	Yes: 15.6%	No: 38.1%		Maybe?: 42.5%	No response: 3.8%

Overall Averaged Grade of Homily: 2.54/4.00, a low C+
Range of Grades Given: One F-,   Five A+

Chart continued on next page

Report Card from the Young Pew, continued

Comments and Recommendations

1. Responses indicate a high level of inconsistency in the quality of Catholic Sunday preaching; that inconsistency did not vary by age group, level of ordination, or geographical locale within the population evaluated.

2. The "person of the preacher" was rated very highly. From the view of the young pew, the formation of "good men" is commendable.

3. The perceived effectiveness of the Sunday homily did not match the perceived quality of the homilist. This suggests that the need for growth in homiletics is skill-based more than formation-based: "Nicer guys" ≠ "More effective homilists." Growth in the basic skills of preaching is needed.

Source: *Are You Talking to Me? A Study of Young Listeners' Connection with Catholic Sunday Preaching*: 561 students participated from seven Catholic high schools: two schools in New York and one school each from California, Maine, Ohio, Louisiana, and Indiana. The average age was 16.2 years old. All students in a particular level of theology class took the survey.

Table 7f

PART THREE

Sharing in the Story of Stories

We have a story to tell. We have a story to tell of a Lover whose Love shines like a beacon on a dusky plain. The story that we have to tell begins with the One who is by nature Storyteller. That story was told long before we had conscious human memory or historical record of it. That story will be told long after each of us is gone. It begins with an invitation, a call, a plea, to each person to enter into that story. It begins with the freedom to give a personal "yes" to that Ultimate Mystery or to shrink away into the "no" of self-contained darkness.

The story of preaching is part of that human story. It is the story of each person's "yes" and each person's "no" to the God who speaks. As we join into the story, to imitate our God, we also speak. We cannot tell the whole story, but we can tell *our* story, our story of the One who speaks. All together, as we speak or as we refuse to speak, we create human history.

The voice of "yes" to God has resounded through acts of faithfulness, deeds of courage, and decisions to love. The first "yes" that we hear came from an aged man in the Middle East four thousand years ago. We hear "yes" from a prophet who put his life at risk to retell the story of the faithful Covenant-Maker. We hear "yes" from a young woman willing to bear the Son of God. We hear an agonized "yes" in a garden with a sweating of blood. "Yes" poured from the pen of an author who burned to put into writing the stories of Jesus. "Yes" erupted from the lips of a martyr just before she was torn to pieces by a lion. "Yes" flowed from a Tongue called Golden who never stopped striving to become more eloquent for the glory of God. A reformed rhetorician swept his audience up into "yes." A little man in a brown robe said "yes" as he lay in the dirt

113

to die. A large round pope said "yes" to the call to open the doors of the church to let the light in. A deacon said "yes" as he preached a young man through his nightmares.

Yet history is not only made up of the recorded "yes-es." Each person's yes or no, in each and every moment, impacts the course of the world. Preaching is broader than a ten-minute homily at a Sunday liturgy: "yes" can be a small act of kindness or a fiery maelstrom of words; it comes through the exuberant "amen" of a First Communicant; it arises with the ancient arthritic who struggles to raise her arm during the Our Father.

The voice of "no" has also resounded through history. Sins of omission, acts of cowardice, and decisions of ignorance and hardness have blocked the preaching of the story. No!" boomed from a Pharaoh who would not let God's people go. "No" roared from religious leaders who had no use for a nobody from Nazareth. "No" played from a rooftop as Rome was burning. A hardened heart said "no" to an indigenous woman's plea for mercy in Paraguay. A low-ranking prelate whispered "no" to an Augustinian monk's early concerns about ecclesiastical corruption. The "no" of a seventeenth-century Japan shogun resulted in the death of thirty-five thousand Christians. The banning of an intellectual religious order said "no" at a critical turning point of scientific questioning. "No" shrank the church from engaging the modern world in the disequilibrium of the Industrial Revolution. "No" echoes today from elected officials who refuse to honor the sanctity of human life.

"No" has changed the course of history in small ways also: the gifted orator who sensed the call to the priesthood but turned away; the decision for one more drink which led to the car accident; the note that never got written; the unwillingness to hear another's point of view; the feedback that was brushed away and the "no" to the listener who was belittled for having given it; the talent overlooked for lack of the correct credentials; the bishop who was afraid to take a risk; the woman who refused to hear, for the fury in her heart; the good man overburdened who was too tired to see clearly. . . . All of this too makes history.[1]

The story of preaching begins with the Story of Stories. Perhaps at two thousand years of church history, we are only at the beginning.[2] We join in by telling our story: I tell my story, you tell your story. Then we listen and with "yes" we act. Or we plug our ears and with "no" we do nothing. We are likely to do some of both. The reign of God is here, but it is also not yet here. To work for the kingdom of God is our noble adventure, to share in that story of stories. So come, together let us go and make history.

We Remember How You Loved Us

Lift up your heads, O gates!
and be lifted up, O ancient doors!
that the King of glory may come in. (Ps 24:7)

The Memory of Presence

On one of my summer days at the University of Notre Dame, as I sat by St. Mary's Lake, I felt the kingdom of God close at hand. I rested my elbows on the picnic table that was chained to the red maple tree. With chin in hand, I sank into contemplation. The ducks squawked. Geese chased each other, noisily splashing into the lake. Runners dashed by on that brilliant July afternoon. The smell of barbequed chicken wafted from the smoke on the patio at Columba Hall, evoking the taste of summer. I sensed that the Creator was at work in the creation. As I looked and listened to that Presence in everyday life, my ribcage swelled, joy overflowed, and I felt a foolish grin widen across my face. Who could I share that with? How was I to put words to that experience of the kingdom? Could I dash to the shore and shout, "Look! God is here!" to the swans and the catfish? How could I keep from singing about this Goodness? How could my words rise like incense before that intimate and infinite Grandeur?

The Story of Stories

There is a story whose memory is at the core of Christian proclamation. The coming of the kingdom of God was at the heart of Jesus' preaching: the good news was that the divine king delighted to reveal himself as a loving father, one who rejoiced to bring his lost children home.[1] The Hebrew Scriptures often spoke of that God-king, that divine ruler (Ps 5:2; Isa 6:5; Isa 41:21): "Lift up your heads, O gates! and be lifted up, O ancient doors! that the King of glory may come in. Who is the King of glory? The LORD, strong and mighty, the LORD, mighty in battle!" (Ps 24:7-8) The king of glory was expected to regather the scattered tribes of Israel. When God came, he would rule in power and all of Israel would come home. Jeremiah and Isaiah prophesied about that future coming (Jer 31:8-10, Isa 51:11).

Like all preachers, Jesus spoke within a particular context: to a con-quered people of (about) AD 30 in a small Roman colony east of the Mediterranean. At the time of Jesus' preaching, the Jews longed for the ten lost tribes of Israel to return. Their fervent hope rested on the coming of the King to liberate them from the power of evil (Ps 5:2, Isa 6:5; 41:21).

Into this milieu of expectant faith strode the carpenter from Nazareth, proclaiming that the "kingdom of God" was at hand. In a voice of au-thority, he implied that he was the agent to effect the coming of God's kingdom: Jesus himself was God's preaching; he himself was the message; he himself was God's revelation.

Why did the unknowable Infinite One come into concrete human reality? It was as though God the Preacher evaluated the connectedness of his own preaching and decided, "My people have not been getting this message. I've got to recast it into a form that they can understand."

Therefore through the incarnation, what Jesus said and what he did flowed together. As he proclaimed the kingdom, he called his hearers to repentance, and at the same time, he healed the sick and fed the hungry. He declared that his miracles and his exorcisms were signs and a fulfillment that the awaited moment had come: "This is the time of fulfillment. The kingdom of God is at hand. Repent and believe in the good news" (Mark 1:15). The people of Israel encountered a taste of glory in this traveling prophet. Expectation was intense.

Here, Yet Not Here

Jesus' teaching about the kingdom held an inherent tension—if the kingdom had come, then why did he not drive out the Romans? Why was there still suffering? Why death? Why pain? The kingdom had come, but the kingdom had also not yet come. The time of fulfillment was not here—Jesus did not know the time or the hour (Mark 13:32). In the prayer that he taught his disciples, he prayed, "Your kingdom come, Your will be done, on earth as it is in heaven" (Matt 6:10). Two apparent contradictions led to a higher truth. Here—but not yet here.

So what happened? Where did this king go? On Palm Sunday, palm branches waved. Children shouted. Lazarus had been raised from the dead

(John 11). The king was here! "Hosanna! Blessed is the one who comes in the name of the Lord! Blessed is the coming kingdom of our ancestor David! Hosanna in the highest heaven!" (Mark 11:9-10).

But the kingdom was not yet fully realized. He who came to give abundant life lost his own. To the distress and dismay of his followers, Jesus died.

Preaching the Paschal Mystery

Happily for Christianity, Jesus did not stay in the tomb. More tastes of glory followed the resurrection and Pentecost events. Timid followers grew bold. Filled with the Holy Spirit and ablaze to proclaim the kingdom, the implicit teaching of Jesus as the agent of salvation became explicit in the preaching of the apostles. The memory of the life, death, and resurrection of Jesus became like a pebble dropped into the water. Like ripples on a lake, the church grew. The proclamation of the Paschal Mystery began to spread throughout the world.

Now we live in the last days, the days between "the Easter event" and the final coming of Christ in glory. For two thousand years, the church has struggled to preach Jesus of Nazareth. The tension remains—the kingdom of God has come, but it has also not yet come. Geese still fight. Young oak trees are overtopped and pulled down by grapevines. Human beings, both inside and outside of the church, do not love each other as we should. Creation groans as we await its fulfillment (Rom 8:22). We remember and we wait and we hope. While we wait, we tell and retell the story.

We Remember, Yet We Forget

In Christian faith, the person of Jesus of Nazareth comes first. From the experience of Jesus, the apostles told what they had seen and heard. The writings of the New Testament arose from that communal telling of the story. Several hundred years of encounter with the God who is Father, Son, and Holy Spirit worked its way into the articulation of the creed. To say it in another way, Jesus Christ is the center of the Christian message. Scripture and Tradition unpack who Jesus is. Church dogmas, doctrines, and disciplines answer the questions, "And what does that mean?" and "How do we put that into practice?"

This encounter with God is primary: it roots itself deeply in our personal and communal memory. Pope Francis speaks of the experience of the gaze of Jesus' love which becomes the believer's ultimate story: "A gaze that makes you develop and keep on going, that encourages you, because it makes you feel that he loves you."[2] This meeting with God comes before the expression of belief and the analysis of belief. Stated in Latin as *lex orandi, lex credendi*, this means that what we *say* that we believe is built upon the *lived experience* of God.

This encounter shows itself in the prayer of the church. The "liturgy is living in that eternal circulation of love within the Trinity."[3] The concrete sights and smells and tastes and touches and sensations, weave memories of living in that eternal circulation of love.

For two thousand years, as we have gathered to pray, the "smells and bells" of liturgy have choreographed a communal experience. Psychological studies now tell us that experience is the foundation for belief.[4] Our understanding of the world arises from the way that we tell our personal stories in our heads.[5] The experience comes first. Belief then arises from what we remember.[6]

The homily is a privileged moment within that liturgy. Why has the church refocused the Tridentine purpose of preaching from simply to teach the faithful what to "believe and do in order to get to heaven"? As we saw in chapter 4, as history changes, preaching also has to change in order to connect with the needs of the people. We have gained the richer understanding that the encounter with God is what fuels those beliefs and those actions. Do we still

> Outer conformity arises from inner assent.

believe in right doctrine and good morals? Certainly. The fruits of belief do not change, but outer conformity arises from inner assent.[7] The focus of *Preaching the Mystery of Faith* is that the purpose of preaching to bring the faithful into encounter with Jesus Christ. The story of the Paschal Mystery comes first. We remember. We believe. We act.

Memory → Belief → Attitude → Behavior

We consider ourselves to be highly logical creatures, yet studies suggest that we are not as rational as we think we are.[8] People construct their worldview through memories. Attitudes arise from those beliefs; behaviors come from those attitudes. In simplified form, story leads to belief, which forms attitudes, which then drives our behavior. To change behavior, then, we go back through the process and recast the mental story. (To test this out, ask someone about their earliest memory of church. Even within the same family, people remember that experience differently, hence their attitude and thus their current behavior may be different. To test this out in another way, watch how political campaigns intentionally craft stories about their candidates [or opponents] in order to drive beliefs about them in order to get your vote.) Experiences and contexts inform what we believe, our attitudes, and thus how we behave.[9]

Our perspective of God comes from the mental images inside our brains. New pieces of information can change that image. Fresh experiences of encounter can recast the mental story. Effective liturgy, for example, works slowly and builds attitudes over a lifetime: the uplift of music, stories about Jesus, preaching that inspires, prayers for unity and of intercession, the intentional forward

> Memory undergirds belief.

movement in the communion line, the assent of holding forth the hand or the tongue, and the call to go out to all the world—all of these come together to craft a personal and communal memory of fidelity to God and God's fidelity to us.

On the flip side, over the long term, lifeless liturgy also works slowly and crafts a different attitude. Preaching that marginalizes or bores, music that is self-absorbed or tonally flat, and a congregation of divisiveness—these form a story which leads to an attitude of another sort.

At this juncture in history, Pope Francis has been recasting the story of what it means to be "church" as the people of God: a people who are in solidarity with the poor in a broad tent where all are welcomed. These are not new Catholic beliefs, but through his word and example, he is telling the story of "church" in a fresh way.[10] Some of those who are on the margins of faith, for whom the news is their source of input, have begun to reframe their own mental stories of "Catholic church" as a result.

Beliefs grow from memories. This principle that memory undergirds belief impacts how we preach, catechize, parent, and evangelize. We each have a responsibility to pass on the story that is at the root of Christian faith. At the same time, we look at the memories of "connection" within the church.

Oneness within the Sheepfold

As we look to connect pulpit and pew in the pursuit of excellence in Catholic preaching, what memories of "connection" are we personally working out of? Our church documents speak of the oneness of the church—one in Christ, one faith, one hope, and one baptism. Do we believe in the oneness of the church? "Of course," we might shrug. Unity is sometimes used as a concept for those "out there" in the relationship to non-Catholic Christian churches.[11] The word "solidarity" is used in social justice documents to describe how we are to treat those who are economically disadvantaged.[12] What about unity and solidarity *within* the church?

If belief is known by its fruits, then the paradox of church life is that we believe and yet we do not believe in the oneness of the church. As we sing "We are one Body," the bricklayer with mortar on his boots may say, "Yeah? Really? That has not been my experience." Oneness is both here and not yet here. We walk out of Mass with a song of oneness running in our brains and then perhaps we hang out only with those who agree with us and demonize those who disagree with us. We believe in solidarity with the poor and then we may not be able to say a kind word to the wealthy widow who sits behind us in the pew. If we are already one, then why do so many of our prayers at Mass pray for unity? Why did Jesus pray for his disciples, "that they may all be one?" Oneness is the premier sign of the presence of the Holy Spirit. The church is to be a living witness of solidarity within a world of discord. The kingdom of God is here, but the kingdom of God is also not yet here.

If the "Holy Spirit is the principle of unity,"[13] what is the concrete reality of our oneness? The kids in my study had much to say about connection with symptoms of comfortableness, the easy flow of laughter and conversation.

As we strive to pass on the story of Jesus the Christ, how, do we make this solidarity a lived reality of church life? As we look to connect pulpit and pew, can we just plug in a program and make it happen? We could. But before we look at structures in the next chapter, if we don't transform existing memories and attitudes, then those programs will be built upon sand as just another Band-Aid program that will not last. We have as much work to do in changing attitudes and healing memories as we do in changing actions. How do we foster unity in parish life? That, too, starts with memory.

The Role of Memory in Breaking Open the Conversation in Catholic Preaching

As a preacher or as one who listens to preaching, if you have no negative memories of Church, this section will not make any sense to you. If you have never experienced discord, been bullied or abused or gossiped about, felt betrayed or messed with or hurt in a parish situation, skip ahead to the next section about listening locally. If you have experienced division or pain, what memory of "oneness" are we personally working out of? As we begin to break open the conversation in Catholic preaching, we have two tasks before us: first, we pray for the healing of negative memories. We cannot open a candid and loving conversation when we are overcome by these emotional weights. What do we do? We ask God for healing. We forgive seven times seventy times. We resolve to start afresh.[14] We remember how God loves us all, yet we also forget.

Second, since the kingdom of God is here but not yet here, we can "complexify our identity."[15] What does that mean? First, we admit that we are not perfect. The story that we tell ourselves about ourselves (personally, as preachers and listeners, and communally as a church) has to broaden. The psychological tendency, when someone points out a need for growth, is to shrink in fear to an all-or-nothing defensive stance of: (1) "Humph. I'm (We're) perfect, what's the matter with you?" or (2) "Wow. I (We) must be real schmuck(s). Thanks for pointing that out." The reality is that we are *much* more complex. We are good, but at the same time we are not yet good. We are travelers on the road toward holiness. The incalculable Spirit continually asks us to grow, personally and communally.

To point toward the need for growth in preaching may be painful in the short term. It will be life-giving in the long term. Healing painful memories and complexifying our identity in the light of God's love will clarify the stories out of which we operate. It will clean out the

> Remember the story—believe we are one—develop an attitude of listening.

"baggage." From there, we will be free to listen. Good preaching and effective reception begins first with an attitude of unencumbered listening.

An Attitude of Listening, Locally

In chapter 2, we looked at data that indicates that sources of influence are coming closer to home. The caring touch of a local community has a great impact on people of faith. At this point in history, "local" makes a difference. Statistically, the strength of the American church is in the parish. Overall, 94 percent of parishioners rate their satisfaction with their parish as good or excellent (58 percent rate it as "excellent").[16] Clergy support their people. Reciprocally, the people support their clergy. "Local" also means "mutual."

The bishops' new document, *Preaching the Mystery of Faith,* may spawn national conferences, diocesan convocations, and regional workshops. But going "far away" is not the only way to strengthen preaching. A preacher's incremental growth can start by getting feedback from the people who listen to it: For the time-pressed, this means to weave homily preparation into the everyday goings-on of the parish. For the weary, this means to imbibe enthusiasm from a community who cares for you. (And take a nap.) For the cash-strapped, this means to interact over a cup of coffee after daily Mass, which is more cost- and time-effective than a weeklong conference.

The homily itself should speak to each unique and local situation. To bring a community into an encounter with God, the homily is not to be a piece of oratorical artwork crafted by a man in his study with his God and his books; it is not to be an isolated event that closes in upon itself, talks to itself, and sits by itself within a eucharistic liturgy; it is not a grand sweeping statement about the mercy of God for all of the world. The goal for the Sunday homily is to be a concrete act of love for a particular community of believers on a specific day in a certain church building.

To make that happen, we break open the conversation locally. Conferences and workshops can be a shot in the arm, but on a day-to-day basis, the parish is where homiletical change can begin.

Each Person Has a Part to Play

What can *you* do? Obviously this is a subject that you care about, or you wouldn't still be reading this book. Every person of every age and every vocational call can begin to pray for the renewal of the Sunday homily. Prayer is powerful. Since there are about a thousand listeners for every man who preaches, then the fruit of a thousand pray-ers can make a difference. We trust that the Holy Spirit wants to renew the preaching of the church. So, first, you and I pray.

Within that prayer for preaching, you also can listen to discern your role in this process of strengthening preaching. As you pray and discern, expect divine creativity. You never know what God will do. The overarching mission is to help each other flourish, whether as preacher or as hearer. So, to break open the conversation about preaching, first seek to understand; then internalize the vision of where we are headed; pray for preachers and their preaching; and then ask the Holy Spirit to lead you in the direction to which *you* are uniquely called: listen, listen, listen, and listen.

Is this culture change possible? Some laypeople feel that it is hopeless. One of the questions in the NCCL survey asked, "As a leader in ministry, how do you suggest that we get to that ideal . . . and what role could you play in making that happen?" One archdiocesan catechetical leader said, "As a layperson, I have no power at all in helping to make this happen." Some experience such a gap between pulpit and pew that connecting the two feels insurmountable. A current of frustration, injustice, and hopelessness flows beneath the surface among some of those in ministry, both clergy and lay. This heaviness is not to be dismissed lightly.

We are called to be healed and to be healers. Discernment of our own role might be the recognition of our need for forgiveness and healing. First listen, heal, and discern. Then look for bright spots.

Identify What Is Already Going On

What good are you already doing? There are many things that strengthen the effectiveness of Sunday preaching. Parents and grandparents share their own faith stories with their children and grandchildren. Some read the Scriptures together in the evening before Mass. Youth ministers prepare young people to receive the good news of the gospel. Priests work on their homiletical abilities and their spiritual life. RCIA team members teach catechumens and candidates to pray. Deacons unpack theological concepts through baptism and marriage preparation sessions. Parishioners listen for God throughout Mass. Catechists fill children's hearts and minds with stories of Bible heroes. Catholic school teachers and principals pass on the vocabulary of faith, relating the gospel to everyday life. In big and small ways, you may be already doing a lot. If it weren't for these supports, the homily could not connect at all.

So, the third step, after prayer and being open to discernment, is to look at what you already do. How could that activity or relationship further connect the pulpit and the pew? Like the "new evangelization," this is not an add-on program but a process of cultural transformation. Rather than doing more, how can we can strengthen what is now in place?[17]

"Smell Like Sheep"

One of the consistant findings in both the study of youth and the study of lay catechetical leaders was the direct correlation between the amount of conversation that surrounded the homily and the quality of that homily. Where conversation about preaching flowed, the homily was well-rated. When there was silence, most often the homily was not well-rated.[18] As a preacher, the more completely you know your people, the fuller the message that you can preach to them. Pope Francis used a similar metaphor when he asked his priests to "smell like sheep": "This I ask you: be shepherds, with the "'odor of the sheep,' make it real, as shepherds among your flock, fishers of men."[19] This is not simply a theological statement of solidarity but also an observation of how to fulfill your ministry.

So what about the conversation that surrounds the homily and the quality of that Sunday preaching? In a few parishes, the talk flows. The homily connects to the lives of the people; there is a good feeling, one of comfort, trust, caring, and the freedom to be oneself, mirroring the symptoms of connection as laid out in chapter 3. How do we get that "flow" going?

Interactions with Parish Staff

A common consensus among lay leaders is that the local conversation is best initiated by clergy themselves. Parish staff can be the first advisers that a homilist turns to for input. (Newly ordained priests, for example, find their most satisfying relationships with the laity with whom they work.[19]) One woman said, "Pastors and deacons need to ask for input. I had one that did that and I think it helped." One homilist told me in an interview that he would check in with his youth minister on Wednesdays as he was crafting his Sunday homily to ask, "What are the kids going through this week?"

These conversations are already happening in a few places. The characteristics of connection come through clearly in this focus group interchange:

> Catechetical Leader: This is the fourth pastor that I have worked with. He, by far, is the best homilist . . . people love to come to hear him. . . . We have a staff meeting on Wednesdays and every staff meeting we share, we pray, we read the Gospel and the readings and then share it . . . his homilies are great . . . he says that he gets inspiration from us. . . . And we didn't do that with the others, the other three.
>
> Interviewer: And were they as good as homilists?
>
> C L: No, no. They had [some] good ones, but he really is *very, very* good. He prays about it, spends a lot of time on it. . . . Even his weddings and funerals, there are no two homilies the same. . . . It is amazing.

In other cases, parish staff members who happen to be in the office may be a resource for the homilist in limited ways: "Once in a while, every blue moon, he'll shout out, 'Who won *American Idol*?' or something like that, because he needs a cultural touch point to make reference to in the homily, and so we'll say, 'So-and-so won that' and then that will show up in the homily as 'This person overcame odds and just won *American Idol'* and that sort of thing . . . like we're his Google."

At other times, the "Loud Silence" among staff members is palpable. Discomfort, self-protectiveness, and distance are described in these interactions: "Interaction/feedback is not sought. It would seem odd to suggest such a thing (though I believe it is needed)." "The tensions in our parish are high, due to the negative feelings between our pastor and congregation (a long story). Our pastor is very unyielding and authoritarian. He is not open to suggestions in most areas. He feels he knows more/better than the congregation, so suggestions are not welcome. He is my boss, so I do not make any suggestions because I don't want to make things worse or jeopardize my job/ministry."

As a resource, those who employed in a parish often have a finger on the pulse of what is going on: 91 percent of those surveyed said that they listen to comments from other parishioners about the homily at least occasionally. Yet here too, the Loud Silence makes itself felt: only one in four of those parish leaders regularly pass those comments on to the homilist. The conversation that goes on in the parking lot tends to stay in the parking lot, even with parish staff.

None of the respondents was able to say that the homilist *always* invites his or her input, though one in nine suggest that it happens frequently. As to integrating the homiletical message into other faith formation efforts in the parish, none (0 percent) could say that "the homilist and I discuss the message and goal of the upcoming homily" always or frequently; 6 percent said that happens occasionally; the other 94 percent said that rarely or never is there any advance consultation about the message or the goals of the preaching. These people are valuable resources. They are being overlooked.

How about coordination of adult and youth faith formation efforts? One catechetical leader suggested that advance planning could synchronize and thus reinforce catechetical themes and spiritual high points. At this juncture, the only time this appears to be (very occasionally) happening is in the context of major sacramental celebrations: First Communion was most commonly mentioned as the point where an integration of the liturgical homily and catechesis occurred. Even though the Sunday homily is the prime source of formation for those not in the inner circle, none of the lay leaders involved in adult faith formation could say that they had any homiletical integration with their efforts (or the reverse).

Frequent and friendly feedback from the folks in the office can begin to strengthen the culture of listening within a parish. Other parish staff members can also help. Parish secretaries are often on the front lines of the "parking lot" conversations about the Sunday homily. The custodial staff frequently has an ear to the ground as well. An organist who faces the assembly during the Sunday homily says, "I witness the 'glaze' in most people's face during the way-too-long homilies. I can tell they (and me) are progressively 'zoning out.' I have heard altar servers describe the same."[20] Homilists, who ask for help from those they work with, often find staff input helpful.

Attend to the Needs in Front of You

What can the ordinary person in the pew do to improve the connectedness of their parish homilies? Folks yearn for a homily that feeds their spiritual hungers. Atkinson, the lay preacher from 1942, described the challenges and the hopes for preaching in his day:

> We don't know much. But we do know what it means to struggle—to marry with a good job, and suddenly be laid off; to get a fine young woman to share life's venture with and then [for her to] be taken desperately ill; to bring into the world five or six fine boys and girls, who are sure that Dad will never fail them, and then have the future turn black. . . . Such trials come to most of us—men and women, young and old—in one way or another; and they bear down hard on the effort to get to heaven. . . . Then it is that your simple, homely talks will delight our minds and make our hearts grow; then it is that silent prayers of thanksgiving will go up to a good God who has brought into our troubled lives a priest who knows how to preach.[21]

How can parishioners hear "homely talks that delight our minds and make our hearts grow?" Many who sit in the pew feel that there is little that they can do about the Sunday homily. Some priests suggest differently: "I can think of no greater service to the pastoral practice of the church than constructive criticism of preaching. If such a movement were to take hold among the people of God, there would be nowhere to hide for the unprepared, the hollow and the offensive."[22]

One priest described how motivating it was to him to have his high school youth group kids sit in the front pew and take notes during his homilies.[23] Preachers have needs too: an interested and engaged audience is stimulating and feeds the speaker. Even a nod of agreement or a smile of response during the homily at the 7 a.m. Mass is helpful; it may encourage the homilist who feels like he is the only creature alive at that time of morning. In one of my clergy interviews, a young priest shared this story:

> I've got a friend who was just ordained last year, who has found his "preaching voice" . . . in the last three months. [He] was trying to figure out how to do this. So when people have told me this that Fr. So-and-so's homilies have gotten better, I asked them, "How they have gotten better?" They told me.
>
> I said, "Please write him a letter or send him an email and tell him: This is what I've seen when you came. . . . I saw you grow and [I] just wanted to encourage you. Your homilies have affected me and/or my family/or the parish in this way."
>
> (It will go a long way because there may not be feedback . . . and a lot of times it may be the same people saying things.)
>
> So I said, "Hey, drop him a line and tell him what you just told me . . . and then I'll follow with a text."
>
> [Later when I saw them, I asked,] "Please, did you write your letter yet?"
>
> "No, I didn't."
>
> "Do it, it's important."

As this priest says, when you see bright spots, encourage, encourage, encourage. Send a card or an email. Clergy gave other suggestions: Be a friend who treats me like a real person, not just someone wearing a robe. Build a relationship of trust. Ask, "How are you?" and mean it. Priests, deacons, and bishops are human beings too. Be aware of their needs.

The "circuit rider" in chapter 5 represented many newly ordained priests when he bemoaned that the first two things to disappear in parish life are time to prepare the homily and moments for uninterrupted prayer. Lay-led finance and pastoral councils, when approached collaboratively, can be of great support so that managerial duties don't overwhelm the spaces needed for homiletical and spiritual preparation.[24] One catechetical leader put it this way: "help priests deepen their spiritual/prayer lives by getting them out from under the pile of administrative duties they never signed up for!"

In addition, laypeople are capable of shouldering parish responsibilities with their clergy, if both sides are fired up to further their parish vision together. I ran into a priest friend from another region of the country and asked him how his parish was doing. He described how he had recently moved into what he called a "self-administering" community. "This is their parish," he said. He enthused about the eleven commissions which were all very active, as well as a peer-run retreat program that had invigorated the spiritual life of the parish. "I'm just here to keep it going," he smiled.

When asked what five things she could personally do, a lay leader responded: (1) I could get over my fear of speaking to "Father" about his homilies; (2) I could pray for this initiative of opening up the conversation about preaching; (3) I could learn how myself, and then train parishioners how to give appropriate feedback so this becomes a healthy interaction; (4) I could learn more and then speak about what makes for effective preaching; (5) I could give it my all.

One catechetical leader already lives St. Paul's vision that we "be of the same mind" (Phil 2:1). In each of her responses to the NCCL survey, she described a rapport with her pastor who is both a good listener and also her boss. His life-giving homilies arise from the consistent give-and-take of feedback and input from staff and parishioners. What did she see as her role in furthering the preaching? She said, "My role in making that happen is to be on the journey myself and affirm/challenge my pastor on his journey."

To listen locally begins with a resolute belief in solidarity, the conviction that "we are all in this together." This, then, leads to an attitude of careful listening to the other. Paying attention to the needs that are in front of us, in turn, leads to the crafting of homilies that speak to our own people. Online homily helps, commentaries, and spiritual reading may have a place in homily preparation, but the local community is a rich and often overlooked source for preaching. The remembrance of how God loves us happens here and now. Those stories sit in our pews. We each have a story to share.

We Remember, We Believe, We Act

In part one of this book, we looked at why preaching matters and to whom. In part two, we looked at the complexities that surround the homily and why Catholic preaching is such an uphill climb—factors of history, clergy life, listener life, and the interaction between pulpit and pew from the words of youth. In this chapter, we have looked at the memory of the reign of God. The local community is the place to tell that story. What is next?

Preaching as an Act of Love within a Milieu of Caring

O Lord, open my lips,
  and my mouth will declare your praise. (Ps 51:15)

Karl Rahner called it, "the silent coming of God."[1] I saw it last Sunday. The deacon preached from the ambo. "Do you believe in miracles?" he asked. Directly in my line of sight beyond him, a ten-year-old altar server listened intently. The boy's back straightened. He raised his chin. His eyes focused on the deacon. His body language revealed his concentration. The homily went on, then the rest of the Mass. When I stood facing the altar before going up to the sanctuary as a minister of communion, the lad once again came into my view. His brown bangs hung straight down; he stared at the marble floor. I thought about his family. He and his three young brothers needed a miracle. His mom had just come home from the hospital three days earlier, and not for the first time: the prognosis was mixed. At "Behold the Lamb of God. Behold him," he raised his head. His face was radiant. His eyes glowed with happiness. Something holy was happening: his heart was on fire with a resounding "yes!" His encounter with God had been sparked by the simple homiletical question: "Do you believe in miracles?"

We have bright spots in Catholic preaching. In every generation, the Holy Spirit comes in unexpected ways.[2] God is at work in the church. If one life has been changed on one particular Sunday, can it happen again? Is the exertion worth it? The evidence from vibrant parishes and renewed faith suggests that focused effort pays off. To fall in love with Jesus through the inner reverberation of the gospel is the promise of the Sunday homily and a primary source of our evangelization.

As we enter into the "Era of Preaching" (as described at the end of chapter 4), there are more opportunities to preach, higher expectations of the homily, and a wider variety of potential types and resources for preaching than ever before.

Envision the Ideal through Prayer

The ideal is lofty: The priest or deacon is a role model for his people. The homilist preaches a message that is iconic as a window into God. The listener cocreates meaning with that word in an encounter graced by the Holy Spirit. The parish together is renewed by that connected experience of light and joy and peace within the context of the eucharistic liturgy. The faith of that community then radiates outward to transform the world in which it lives so that the culture grows ever more godly. The church is to be a locus of passion, enthusiasm, and gospel adventure as a source of hope for the world.[3] That is the vision. That is what we work for.

Moving from the lofty to the particular, how does that noble idea work in practice? How is that expectation to be met by a man who every week may preach two funerals, a wedding, four daily Masses, and a baptism in addition to two or three services on a Sunday? "Preacher fatigue" can be very real.[4] How is that expectation to be met by listener who feels time-pressed, burdened with cares of family and finances, school and social demands, surrounded by a world of nonbelief and noncommittal? "Work fatigue" is also very real.[5] Holding up that dream as a standard could make an overwhelmed homilist even more whipped by the end of the day. Offering that model could exhaust the already harried human in the pew. Yet as we pray for preaching, we envision the ideal through God's eyes. If we don't have a vision, how do we know where we are headed?

One Step at a Time

We have unpacked the complexities of the homiletic encounter from historical, clergy, and listener viewpoints. In the last chapter, we have a story to tell, factors of memory and healing, and developing an attitude of listening locally. We have now built at least a rudimentary understanding of where we stand in Catholic preaching. So now what? Within a world of reduced energies and limited time and restricted budgets, how can we move from where we are, to where we would like to be? What concrete steps do we need to take? What do we *do* about Catholic preaching in the local parish?

I suggest three things that are needed to bring about this local cultural change: (1) a clear prayer-inspired vision of where we as a parish want to be in our Sunday preaching; (2) opening the parish conversation to: (a) develop an understanding of the current situation; (b) grow a deep-seated belief that this change is necessary; (c) find the motivation to make that change a priority; and (3) set up well-supported structures to make that change happen. None of these steps will work alone. Without a change in mindset, new-found ways of acting are transitory and do not last. Without a change in habits, new attitudes and beliefs will not be reinforced; the memories of that new way of acting will fade away. Without structural support, this book is just one more happy thought that ends up in the bargain bin of history. Each of these steps is needed to make this cultural change happen.

Setting Up Structures for Preaching Conversation

The last chapter advocated for each individual reader, whether listener or preacher, to pray and discern about what to do about Catholic preaching. If you are a layperson and you have been reading this book by yourself, gather a group together to read and discuss the conundrum of connection in Catholic preaching. Then pray and heal and discern in what direction the Holy Spirit is calling you to strengthen the preaching in your particular sphere of influence.

As a layperson, what if you have no idea how to begin to break open this conversation? What if the Loud Silence infests your parish culture so acutely that an antidote seems out of reach? What if the tastes of solidarity that others have described have made you want to cry with longing because at this point your community is nowhere near that kind of connectedness? If that is the case, give a copy of this book to those who preach in your parish or diocese. To overcome the perception gap about how much preaching matters, it is vital for the laity to make more noise—to continually communicate how life-giving the Sunday homily could be for you and for those you love.

If you are a homilist and a stack of twelve copies of *Connecting Pulpit and Pew* have arrived on your desk in the last two months, this might be an unspoken suggestion that your people would like to help you with your preaching, but they do not know how. Start a study group. (After all, you will already have the copies in hand.) Read, discuss, pray, and discern together.

As a local community, you can then pray together to ask the Holy Spirit to show you how to make this vision happen in your own time and space. To recap the vision, here is what you are looking for: Listeners take co-responsibility for their parish preaching. The homily is to be an act of love within a community of caring (as a mutual caring for the preacher and the preacher caring for them). The homily leads the people to encounter God. The faithful then get fired up to go out and transform the world in which they live.

How do you get there? It begins with conversation and prayer. The processes will inculturate differently for each parish or diocese because needs and personalities are different. As the quality of listening and discernment increases, so will the creativity in the initiatives that you design to strengthen your local preaching.

If you, as people of both pulpit and pew, have read through this book together as a group and you are reading this very last chapter, where do you go from here? Hopefully, you have talked and laughed and prayed and worked through the discussion questions in the back of the book, and you have a pretty good handle on the strengths and struggles of preaching in your own community. The next natural step, then, is to move from being a study group to become a preaching preparation team.

Setting Up Structures to Work Together

The 1982 USCCB document *Fulfilled in Your Hearing* suggested lay preaching preparation teams: "An effective way for preachers to be sure that they are addressing some of the real concerns of the congregation in the homily is to involve members of that congregation in a homily preparation group"[6] That thirty-year-old document gives an outline of how to structure each session of that preparation group. Pick up a copy and follow it. This is not a new idea; many who have tried these groups have found them to be helpful. Chatteris says, "A preaching committee can help a preacher to discern a congregation's needs and thus assist in finding helpful themes for homilies. Such a group can also break down the alienating sense of loneliness that can accompany the process of preparing homilies, an awful feeling of flying solo."[7]

Preaching preparation groups had their day in the sun after the authoring of *FIYH*, but did not then become a permanent structure within parish life. Perhaps in the push for the new evangelization, they could be resurrected as an expectation for a fresh generation of preachers? Shea describes it this way: "Most of us tend to preach in a vacuum where we are forced to assess our own preaching and draw conclusions using the few tidbits of input that we only casually and informally receive. We preach without the benefit of concrete feedback that could make a radical difference in what and how we preach."[8]

Acts of solidarity within the church will strengthen our belief in solidarity: building positive memories of pulpit and pew working together will further the attitude that working together is a healthy and not a fearful, step forward for preaching.

Listening skills are integral to effective preparation groups: "Although preaching is often referred to as 'breaking open the Word,' that is only half of the task. The other half is allowing ourselves to be broken open by the word, letting scripture expose our weaknesses, our inadequacies, our need for grace, as well as the love of God that is already present in our midst."[9]

Within a feedback group, tread carefully. Remember, preaching is a sensitive issue and feelings and identity are at stake. When a parishioner makes a comment about the homily, it may have taken much courage for him or her to say anything. If a priest or deacon asks for feedback, it may have taken much courage to ask for it. Both clergy and lay may have memories of times when feedback has gone badly, and as a result, he or she feels hesitant to broach the topic again.[10]

On the flip side, a culture of silence is also not healthy. When homilists are left to guess how they are doing, this can foster the maladaptive behaviors of avoidance, blame, and self-exaltation/degradation/justification, as well as disappointment and frustration. One eighty-seven-year-old former pastor sighed, "When people left my parish, they never came by to tell me why. How was I supposed to know?" Comments have to be clear, concrete, and specific, within a rapport of trust. Encourage, be gracious, and be tactfully truthful. Preaching preparation teams can be rotated frequently so that a broad range of parishioners "buy into" and help with the homiletic message.

> Comments have to be clear, concrete, and specific, within a rapport of trust. Encourage, be gracious, and be tactfully truthful.

Other Structures Already in Place

Other structural opportunities come from the use of existing parish groups as advisory teams.[11] Clergy support groups can strengthen their preaching together; each could bring spiritual input from their parishioners. District meetings, which often include both clergy and lay staff, are another source for reflection and input on the upcoming preaching (though the "business" may overwhelm that schedule).

One catechetical leader described one such source of input for the homilist: "Although it is not necessarily for homiletic discussion, our monthly staff and pastoral council meetings use reflection and sharing on the upcoming Gospel as our prayer experience, so the Pastor hears other voices." A leader in a large suburban parish obviously enjoyed the wealth of input from his people through exchanges in parish meetings:

> The other thing we do, in terms of preparation, which I like, is that all the organizational meetings that happen here during the week reflect on the Scripture of the week to come. So, from staff meeting to parish council to whatever other group meeting, I ask that their prayer include one of the readings . . . that way, it sort of allows me to be a little bit more lazy *(much laughter)*, because I can steal all the reflections from staff or from another meeting, in terms of what people are thinking about and how they are interacting with it. . . . So, instead of me just being alone in my room with a couple of books, you're getting, "What is the staff thinking about, related to this reading?" "How do they hear it?" "What are they getting out of it?" as Fr. [ ] (one of our homiletics professors) said, "When it comes to homilies, steal everything you get your hands on." Which is true, you know *(more laughter)*.

First Do No Harm

What if the preaching is not going well in your parish? What do you do? As a preacher, whose definition of "well" are you working out of? When 82 percent of priests consider themselves to be above-average preachers, complacency can creep in. Good enough is, well, good enough.

Is the bland leading the bland better than the blind leading the blind? One lay leader said, "In my previous parish the pastor used a lot of higher criticism of the Bible, which is like acid to the faith. So I am grateful that my current pastor just gives 'nice' warm-feeling homilies that have little substance. At least he is not causing people to reject basic tenets of Catholicism." Perhaps the Hippocratic Oath of "First Do No Harm" should be taken at ordination, especially for preaching at funerals and other occasions where listeners are highly fragile. Lifelong Catholics sometimes have high hopes but low expectations for preaching.[12]

Those who join the church from other Christian denominations may have a broader experience of the Sunday message. Some of the greatest advocates for preaching improvement are those who have joined the

Catholic Church as adults. In my own Presbyterian upbringing, I sat at the feet of a superb preacher throughout my adolescent years; therefore it takes a *lot* for me to say that the Catholic preaching that I hear is "excellent."[13] Lifelong Catholics perceive preaching differently from those who have entered the church later in life. So who is to say what makes for "good" preaching in parish conversations?

What if the Sunday homily is poor and no one has ever been honest with the preacher about it? (One lay leader said, "If the homilies really had an impact on peoples' lives—we would have standing room only in our churches. Today folks vote with their feet.") Parish groups may be hesitant to be open about the quality of the preaching, especially when the "parking lot" conversation agrees that the homilies leave much to be desired. The people may love their homilist but not his homilies. In this situation, a private discussion between clergy and lay may be preferable to an open study group.[14] Even there though, because of the lingering two-tier system, candor may be difficult: you just don't say those things to "Deacon" or "Father" or "Bishop."

So how can we breathe greater transparency into the system? How can we be more objective? If *Fulfilled in Your Hearing* set the purpose of preaching to be "a scriptural interpretation of life," how are we to appraise "interpretation?" What is excellence in preaching?

Structuring Ongoing Assessment

Preaching the Mystery of Faith (2012) both supports and furthers the vision of *Fulfilled in Your Hearing* (1982). In the last thirty years, the writings of John Paul II and Benedict XVI increased the church's emphasis on relationship.[15] The stated purpose of preaching in the new document is to bring the people into an encounter with Jesus Christ. Therefore the bar for preaching has been set even higher. If "you will know them by their fruits," what fruits of encounter are measurable? From the faith growth responses in chapter 7, how have our people "seen" or "touched" or "tasted" God? How have they grown in understanding who God is? How have they changed their beliefs or attitudes or behavior as a result of the Sunday homily? What kind of loyalty and commitment has the homily stirred up in them? For the Catholic world, this has the potential to be an exciting new field of inquiry for scholars and practitioners alike.[16]

If you are a preacher, then, who is encountering God through your words? And how is that happening? If you want to know, you will have to ask. To get a consistent response, like getting a haircut or an oil change, you will have to ask on a regularly scheduled basis.

One priest said that he would like to give a test at the end of Mass. How do you do that? Once per month put a postcard in the pew that asks, "How did you (or did you not) encounter God in the homily that you just heard?" or "What main point will you take home from this homily?" or "What need of yours did this homily speak to?" (Don't worry about dangling participles; apparently it is now okay grammatically to do that.) Listeners can then drop the card in the collection basket.

Once a year on a scheduled day, the whole parish can offer an evaluation of the ways that they have grown (or not grown) in faith as a result of the preaching. This can identify areas of strength and needed growth in connecting with the needs of the people.

A preaching team itself can also use a rubric to increase the objectivity of their analysis of the previous Sunday's homily. Specific people from that group can take the lead in forming a data entry and analysis team and discuss the collated results to the preacher.

Careful design of evaluative tools will foster preaching that connects with the people.[17] Structuring consistent surveys of listeners in a parish setting will unearth a broader range of voices. When parishioners are asked to evaluate, they are more alert. When preachers are evaluated and held accountable, they will devote more time and focus to their preparation. That is only human: "There will be a test" means that we pay more attention.[18]

Incremental Change for Exponential Growth

Once you have this feedback, then what do you do with the results? With objective standards for excellence, a homilist and his preparation team can then structure goal-setting into his annual plan, setting one or two attainable goals each year for continual improvement. Over a lifetime of preaching, especially if the preacher starts young and makes this an unfailing pattern of his ministry, that will make a huge impact on the faith growth of his people. A small change in the quality of the Sunday preaching can result in exponential growth in the church. Why? In what other live venue does a speaker have the opportunity to inspire the same two thousand people (or so) every single week? A Catholic priest or deacon or bishop is like a rock star in the size of his weekly "audience." Even small improvements will create an outward ripple of spiritual growth. (The reverse is also true—increasingly lackadaisical efforts will create a different sort of "moving out" effect.) Chrysostom said that effective preaching comes through hard work and constant cultivation. With objective assessment, some preachers may be surprised to find areas of weakness which they did not know about (and in the cultural Loud Silence, nobody had told them about).

The ability to preach does not come automatically with ordination, nor does elocution come with "the apparent effortlessness of gods."[19] No matter how many times "Good homily, Father" is said at the door, no preacher is ever done improving. (One of the best youth-rated preachers was one of the oldest homilists.) Between clergy and lay, we are not done until the whole world has encountered God and the kingdom of God has come. That will be at the end of time.

Opening the Conversation More Broadly

The focus of this book has been to break open up the conversation about preaching at the local parish level, with love and care. Yet each parish sits within a broader church context and thus is influenced by what goes on in the diocese, the nation, and the world. Therefore, opening the conversation more broadly will also benefit local homiletical interactions. What more is there to say?

The Need for Preaching Research

Preaching research is barely in its infancy. There are many questions. One of the beauties about the earliest studies in any discipline is that we move from the blank slate of "we don't know anything about this" to identify specific questions that need to be asked.

Twenty-five research questions are listed here. They range from a recommendation of a national study of preaching to determine our areas of greatest need; to evaluations of the methods and means to effect ongoing formation in preaching; to identifying pathways to listener understanding; to measurements of seminary homiletics training in relationship to bringing listeners into an encounter with God. As we embark upon this new adventure of preaching for the purpose of an encounter with God, we do not know how encounter happens or how the homily helps the faithful to get there. In order to serve the local parish, that is a wide open and potentially exciting field for homiletics research.

What about the "people" questions? Sometimes we assume that if we could just change one contributor to the system, the whole interaction would be fixed: if only we could change the pastor, the parish would be lovely; if the people would just pay attention, I would preach more effectively; if the bishop would just . . . , etc., etc., etc. To be effective,

National Research and Planning Needs in Preaching
(Rather than assume we know, let us go and find out.)

A. Determine an overall assessment of where we are:

1. How are we doing? Nationally representative studies of the quality of U.S. Catholic preaching—both horizontal and longitudinal (five to ten years).

2. How are we growing/not growing in faith through preaching? Nationally representative study of the long-term impact of Catholic Sunday preaching on faith growth, determining which elements of preaching further the encounter with God, which block that encounter.

B. Strengthen the understanding of the listener:

1. What do people hear? Determine the correlation between the message sent and the message received: subjective and objective understanding of the listener.

2. What does it mean to preach for encounter? Are there consistent fruits that arise from an encounter and how can we measure for that? What elements contribute to effectiveness in bringing our people into a relationship with God? What elements drive people away? What motivates? Maintains attention? What does "bored" mean?

3. Parishioner spirituality: what do our people value? What are their needs for spiritual growth? What are their catechetical/doctrinal needs? How do we speak to their needs for spiritual growth? How much of the weight of those needs can the homily carry? What are other venues for meeting those needs?

C. Strengthen the understanding of the preacher:

1. What are the overall strengths and weaknesses of our preachers in general? What are the sources of the inconsistencies in our preaching? Which preaching skill weaknesses need to be targeted first? Where can we make incremental change that will result in exponential growth?

2. What assessments are effective in analyzing individual strengths and weaknesses in furthering the encounter of preaching? What is the clergy response to those assessments? What are the results of pilot projects in preaching improvement?

3. What motivates change in preaching preparation habits? What sustains that change so that it becomes a way of life?

4. As a man of communion, what factors influence a preacher's listening abilities? How can we identify role models/best practices for listening; what habits create an openness to the needs of the people?

5. What are best practices/models in preaching conversation for the long-term growth of a parish community?

6. How do we encourage spiritual growth in preaching? How do we encourage growth in the skills of preaching?

D. Strengthening the rewards system for "Why improve?"

1. What is the impact of the quality of preaching on the decision to enter the seminary? Determine the role of preaching in the decision toward ordination, especially among youth between ages 12 and 18.

2. What is the impact of the quality of preaching on Mass attendance and the collection basket? Determine the correlation between the quality of Sunday preaching and parish finances, attendance, engagement, and growth.

3. What feedback helps? Determine which parishioner feedback practices foster homiletic growth; which hinder improvement in preaching.

E. Assess Long-term Training Needs for Effective Preaching

1. Evaluate the effectiveness of seminary homiletics programs in relation to their subsequent effectiveness in bringing parishioners into an encounter with God (as a long-term longitudinal study).

2. Evaluate seminary programs to determine the integration of the overall curriculum into the formation to preach; if biblical studies have borne fruit, where are systematic theology, pastoral counseling, moral theology, and church history in relationship to the formation of homilists?

3. Determine the most effective means for transmitting ongoing preaching improvement training to clergy according to their stated needs.

4. Identify potential ways to expand the available cadre of preaching coaches and consultants, especially at the MA level.

5. Identify role models of preaching for encounter and determine how to promulgate those models. How can we set up a system of mentors and models of effectiveness?

6. How can we develop guidelines and standards for quality control? How do we ensure accountability and consistency in preaching?

continued

F. Assess Institutional Support Structures for Preaching

1. What structures, approaches, and strategies are in place to support growth in preaching; at the parish, diocesan, and national levels?
2. What structures and mindsets hinder our ability and willingness to connect the pulpit and pew?
3. What structures in parish life hinder preaching preparation and spiritual growth and what changes do we need to make so that preaching becomes a time priority?

a cultural change has to transform the overall system. Each person has to take responsibility for his or her own sphere of influence. This brings up the people questions about which currently we have no data: Why do those who *could* help, keep silent? Why do those who could use help, not ask for it? What implicit reward/disincentive systems are we working out of? What structures, policies, and processes permit poor or erratic performance, and what would it take to change them? And how can we encourage conversation at all levels?

My own search to unearth the current situation of Catholic preaching is a piece of this beginning. Growth occurs when we are not afraid to look at our institutional strengths and our weaknesses. What is needed in homiletics is a dedicated and well-funded research center to ascertain how to effectively connect the gospel message with our people. Even from the preliminary list of questions, there is much to do.

Consistency between Parishes

Chapter 7 contained a brief summary of the quantitative results from my doctoral study. What other overall findings did this set of studies bring to light?

First, we lack consistency in the quality of our Catholic preaching.[20] In some parishes, the preaching is effective and resonates with the needs of the people. In other places, it seems deaf to those connections. A diocesan catechetical leader sees this discrepancy among parishes in practice out in the field. He says,

> I believe the greatest challenge is encouraging homilists to listen
> to the desires, hopes, thoughts, and challenges of the people in
> the pews. I have the privilege (and challenge) of being in dozens

of parishes each year, and the quality of preaching and liturgical celebration runs the gamut. There are places of hope and inspiration, and some of poor quality, lackluster "celebration," and faulty theology. One of the distinctions that I observe between those two extremes is that often the parishes with wonderful Sunday experiences are parishes in which the preachers listen to the people.

To explain this spottiness in our preaching, we often attribute these pockets of connection to character: "He has a gift" is bandied about in conversations about effective preachers. Certainly innate talent is one element of preaching competence.[21] But most of the people in the pew are not yearning for a five-course meal created by a master chef. A peanut butter sandwich that is lovingly prepared for them (and with them) would satisfy their hungers. Both preaching and listening can be learned.

When you enter into a fast-food restaurant to order a spicy chicken sandwich, you expect that particular chicken sandwich to be the same chicken sandwich in Oregon as in Maine. If it is not, you wonder what the district manager is doing to ensure accountability in chicken sandwich making. So we can ask, in a similar way, how does effective preaching become a reliable element of Catholic parish life? Rather than being personality-based and highly unpredictable in quality, how do we incorporate consistency, accountability, and broad-based effectiveness in our Sunday preaching?

This book began by describing the conundrum of connection with the outside world. It closes with the conundrum of connection inside the Catholic world. From words of the pope to the ninth grader in the pew, we all agree that preaching needs to be improved. We can all hope that it will. We can each do our part to make that happen in our respective worlds. Where does preaching improvement fit in the church?

Suggestions from the Field

Diocesan and national lay leaders made up about half of those who responded to the NCCL study. Their answers were more institutionally-oriented than parish-based. They saw a unique opportunity for diocesan departments to collaborate about the improvement of Sunday preaching. The homily sits at the conjunction of liturgy and worship, catechesis and evangelization, parish life, ministries of acculturation, and ongoing formation for clergy.[22] The homily is an integrating moment for all of these disciplines, a place to invite disparate groups to work together.

Sometimes the political dynamics of a diocesan or national office cautions one department to be careful not to invade another's turf. This silo mentality showed up in comments about a desire to help with preaching but a hesitancy to step on toes: "I couldn't do anything unless I was invited. If I were invited, I would jump in with both feet if I were asked."

Lay leaders' readiness to help was consistent. Another offered, "I would be willing to serve as a sounding board and reviewer. . . ." The tone, especially in private conversations, was cautiously hopeful. Not one of these leaders said that Sunday preaching was "not my problem." It impacts them personally. They (and their families) listen to it every Sunday.

The theologically educated laypeople who sit in our pews hear many more homilies than their bishops and priests do. They know the theological world. They live and breathe the experience of the listener. They know that we need help. They want to help.

From these diocesan and national leaders' comments, their responses coalesced into seven suggestions for their bishops:

1. Initiatives are most effective when they come from the bishops first.[23]

2. Require (as in all other professions) ongoing formation of clergy.

3. Encourage conversation at all levels to understand where people are and what they are thinking.

4. Make sure that those who preach are themselves evangelized and understand their part in forming disciples.

5. Invest time and resources into preaching improvement in ways that will make a difference; not scattershot in the hope that something will take root, but based on good data with carefully created initiatives.

6. Create diocesan structures for assessment and accountability and/ or bring in outside theological and communications consultants to assess and support homilists, as you would with a financial auditor or facilities consultant.

7. Strengthen your own homilies so that you model preaching that leads your people into an encounter with Jesus Christ.

John Paul II called for "new ardor, new expressions, and new methods" in the church. The goal is for the faithful to grow fervent in holiness, which will spur them to share their faith with others in a life-giving way. As the fifteenth century teaches us, pockets of preaching reform can make a difference, but full-scale renewal has to come from the top. Like that century, we are in a similarly new cultural situation. For them, it was the printing press; for us, it is the internet. Sources of authority are changing. Diocesan and national lay leaders urged their bishops "to provide episcopal support, encouragement and example for the improvement of preaching."

Preaching as a Priority

Preaching is the first task of priests.[24] We have seen that within the context of the Sunday Eucharist, the homily is the prime source of formation for the people of God. Crafting the homily is the one piece of the liturgy over which clergy have complete control. Preaching's potential for inspiration, conversion, and transformation has been discussed in parking lots and over dinner tables and throughout this book. Preaching matters.

At the same time, the Catholic homiletics world is very small: the annual meeting of the Catholic Association of Teachers of Homiletics (CATH) meets in a church basement around a square of six tables, a gathering smaller than many pastoral council meetings. Only one school in the world provides doctorates for people to be teachers of Catholic preaching. Many of those who teach seminarians to preach are not themselves trained to teach homiletics. So is Catholic preaching a priority for us or is it not?

As we have repeatedly seen, our documents say "yes." Our time and energy and personnel and financial outlays say "no." Catholic books on preaching are numbered in the dozens, compared to hundreds and hundreds of books on saints, sacraments, prayer books, doctrine, and history. The financial outlay for the unfolding of the bishops' new document on preaching was dwarfed by the expenditure to unfold the new *General Instruction of the Roman Missal* (GIRM). In the past ten years, preaching centers have closed for lack of money or participants or leadership. *Preaching* magazine has gone out of business. Money seems to flow into some Catholic enterprises like the Mississippi River, whereas the investment in homiletics is like the trickle of an intermittent stream in a dry Montana autumn. There is little investment in preaching.[25] How can the Sunday homily become a priority? It will take vision, commitment, courage, willpower, financing, and leadership.

Stories Still to Be Told

This book has been a story of stories: accounts of Jesus the magnetic preacher; young peoples' experience of the preaching that they hear; lay and clergy insights into the current homiletical situation; and my own search for connection in preaching. As we begin to open up this conversation in the broader church, there are still more than a billion tales waiting to be told. Each person of faith has his or her own story to tell about the encounter with God through preaching.

As I was eating lunch one day in our seminary cafeteria, a recently ordained priest sat down next to me. We began to talk about preaching and its potential impact on young people. He shared his story: He had been in second grade. When he listened to his priest's homily, something stirred inside his eight-year-old heart: *that* was what he wanted to do when he grew up. Twenty years later, from the eagerness in his voice, it is clear that preaching the gospel is still his passion.

This drama is not our own. Every generation somehow discovers faith anew. Building from our Jewish heritage, we believe that God continues to work in human history. The story is not over. The kingdom has not yet come. The hope for that seven-minute string of words at the eucharistic liturgy is that it will cooperate with the Holy Spirit to transform one person's life this Sunday. That in turn, will change history.

We have a story to tell. We preach the story of stories, the Paschal Mystery of the death and resurrection of Jesus Christ. That preaching is an act of love within a milieu of caring. We can never give up striving for excellence in building a community of solidarity to pass on that message. There is no effort too good for the faith of our people. There is no effort too good for the One who is Storyteller.

As one diocesan catechetical leader said, "Let's continue to work on the issue. It is vital to our future as a church." We have homiletical work to do, together. Jesus prayed that we all be one. Let us be listening.

Epilogue

One of my favorite interchanges in this research process came when I tried to explain to a sixteen-year-old girl how Catholic preaching has changed in the last fifty years. I told her that after Vatican II, the homily became an integral part of the Mass. She lowered her brow in bewilderment and gave me a quizzical look, as though to say, "What's the big deal? Of course the homily is part of the Mass." What was novel fifty years ago is no longer news. The innovation has become a given.

In that same way, the purpose of this book is to put myself out of business. In thirty years, a young priest will shrug, "Certainly we preachers listen to the needs of our parishioners. We know how much the homily matters to them." A bishop will shake his head in amazement, "You mean there was a time when clergy did not feel supported by their higher-ups in their preaching efforts?" A young parent will opine, "We always give our homilist feedback. We want him to connect to us with credibility and fervor."

Those who listen will love those who preach. Those who preach will love those who listen. The homily will be an act of caring within the solidarity of saints. The parish will be the locus of human connection in an even higher-tech world, and the people will burst forth from Mass, happy to share the preached Word of God with their family and friends and neighbors. The church will overflow with people who seek for prayer and reverence and an encounter with God, and their hearts will be filled. Those who look in from the outside will say, "Wow. See how they love each other!" And that sixteen-year-old girl's granddaughter will roll her eyes and give her grandmother a quizzical look and say, "What's the big deal? It has always been this way."

When this cultural shift has become a given, that generation will read the thoughts in this tome and shrug, "Huh, duh, obvious," and toss it into the recycling bin or delete it from their reading device. And I will slide my creaking bones into a sleeping bag in a tent in the darkness of a

Sierra Nevada night, to bask in the light of the stars and pray with Blessed John XXIII, "Lord, it's your church. I am going to bed." And life will be good because God is good; for the Living-One-who-is-a-Communion-of-Love-who-Continually-Wants-to-Share-that-Oneness-with-Us has always been this way.

Questions for Reflection
and Discussion

1 To Encounter God, Together

1. The first chapter tells several stories of growth in faith through preaching. How does preaching make a difference for you? Have you grown in faith as a result of the preaching that you have heard? Describe what that was like.

2. Preaching is a topic that we are not talking about. Describe your reaction to the "Loud Silence." What has been your experience? What are the barriers to having this conversation?

3. As we search for understanding in preaching, what questions do you have? What do you not know? Grow in awareness of your own "sample of experience." How do you see the world that surrounds the homily? What bias does that give you?

4. As a springboard for discussion, who could you share this book with? What are your hopes for that sharing?

2 Preaching and the New Evangelization

1. Chapter 2 says, "Build a church culture that listens and self-evaluates and continually strives for both holiness and competence in our ability to communicate the gospel message." What is your reaction to that statement?

2. John Paul II suggested "New ardor, methods and expression in the 'new evangelization.'" Are we asking the right questions about how we connect with the world in which we live? What are we not seeing? Ask that question of someone who is not in the parish "inner circle" and see what they have to say.

3. Find someone with whom to play the tapping game. Tap out a tune and ask the person to guess what is in your head and switch roles.

As you have learned about the Curse of Knowledge, where do you see it happening? In ordinary life, when have you experienced that syndrome at work?

4. What is your experience of the varying populations who listen (or don't listen) to homilies? Do you have people in your life in those different populations? How much does the preaching matter to their faith growth? What circle do you fit into and who do you hang around with? How does that affect how you see the Sunday homily?

5. As we talk about the weight of negative memories, what is one of your earliest negative memories? Why has that stuck with you? Why does it weigh so heavily?

3   Not Made to Be Alone

1. What does "connect" mean to you? When have you experienced it? Who have you most connected with in your life?

2. Describe a moment of disconnection. What were the symptoms of that?

3. Think of someone with whom you do not connect well. Which of the pathways to connection would be most fruitful for you to explore? What is one thing that you could do to strengthen that connection?

4. Sometimes it is challenging to connect with a person who is not like you, especially when you are dissimilar in matters of faith (which are very deeply held). Even if you have differences, what points of connection do you have in common with that person? Where can you find a starting point? What *could* you talk about (or do) that would build a connection?

5. What does it mean to "connect pulpit and pew" as in connecting theology to life? How do we speak of God in words that another understands?

4   Surrounded by the Greats of History

1. As a listener, what is your own personal history with preaching? If you are currently a homilist, what is your experience of listening to the preaching of others? Describe each as concretely as you can.

2. What was the preaching like when you were a child? How does that memory form your beliefs about and expectations of preaching now (as a listener) or (as a homilist)?

3. Imagine that you have just gotten to heaven. Which of the historical preachers would you like to meet? Why? What is it about that preacher that appeals to you?

4. God as Revealer has been involved in all of history. What is your story? Where do you "see" God in the history of your life?

5. The purpose of looking at history is to learn from the past. The world is in the midst of a change. What are the needs for preaching today? How do we reach out to those needs? What kind of preaching do you think will make a difference in the world of today? (If the group does not agree with each other, what different memories and samples of experience are you working from?)

6. What are your hopes for the future of the homily? If the Sunday preaching were the very best that it could be, what would that look like? How would it impact you, your family and friends?

5   Painting a Picture of God

1. Describe the personal satisfactions that you find in ministry. If you are clergy, describe those satisfactions. If you minister in other ways (we all are ministers in some way, whether to family or friends or coworkers), describe what you find satisfying. Where is the Sunday homily among those satisfactions?

2. How did the description of "co-culture" resonate with your experience, as clergy or as layperson? What can we do to intentionally create more points of "connection"?

3. What did you learn from this chapter? What made you resist or "push back"? Was there one point where you found yourself rationalizing, excusing, justifying, or blaming either yourself or your preacher? How do you see your own communication abilities? How do others see those abilities? Ask them.

4. Where is God at work in clergy culture? Where do we need renewal?

5. As a homilist, look at your own preaching preparation. Which of the factors surrounding the homily most impact "doing your homework"? What can you do about it? How much energy and motivation do you have to make that change?

6. In an interview, one pastor said that he never hears anything from his people (who incidentally, love him very much). What he would like to hear is this: "Tell me what helps you to grow to understand God's word; to grow in faith; to be more inspired. What is the most

inspirational homily that you have heard me give?" Encourage your homilist with a story of even the smallest moment of growth.

6 The World of the Listener

1. What do you see as the joys and struggles of lay life? How do these affect the Sunday homily?

2. Describe the holiest person that you have ever met. Is this an ordained or a lay person? What makes the person so holy? How does the person behave that makes you believe in his or her holiness? What is one thing that you could do to be like this person?

3. Where do you get your sources of information about the secular world in which we live? How often do you watch the news or check the internet for what is happening "out there"? How accurate is that as a source of information about the people among whom you live and breathe?

4. Where and how God is "speaking" in moments of beauty, moments of duty, moments of camaraderie—the fruits of the Spirit are love, joy, peace, patience, kindness, goodness, faithfulness, gentleness, self-control. Is God there, even in nonreligious settings, when you see those fruits?

5. Where is God at work in our secular culture? Where do we need renewal? Do you believe that there is a battle of good versus evil going on, and if so, who do you believe will "win" this game? At the same time, do you see the beauty in our culture? What are the encouraging spots in lovely lay life? How can we name and strengthen those positives?

7 Connecting with Sunday Preaching and the Sunday Preacher

1. From their words in chapter 7, young people would like Sunday preaching to speak to them. What do you do that might be interesting to a high school youth? What do you and they have in common?

2. What does it mean to you to "put your ear to the ground"? What is one way or one place that you could do that better? When you get together with others, how often do you do the talking/teaching? How often do you do the listening/receiving?

3. What do you do, as layperson or as clergy, to connect with young people in a casual way? Do they see you often in a nonauthoritative role? As parents, grandparents, priest, deacon, bishop, friend, do you "hang out" and make yourself available to them on their terms (in a Virtus-appropriate way, of course).

4. As you look at the "Report Card from the Young Pew," what stands out for you? In which elements do we need the most work? How can you help with that?

8 We Remember How You Loved Us

1. As Christians, we believe that the kingdom of God is here. That is the source of our preaching, whether in our own personal life or from the pulpit. Where have you experienced that God has "pitched his tent among us?" Name five little things that reveal God to you. Name three ways in your life in which you see that the kingdom of God is both here and has not yet come.

2. The actions of all people, when combined, are together what make history. Those compiled actions may not individually make the reference books, but they do form the history of the human race. Each person's action also informs the history of other people's lives. As a person who makes history, how can you be a preacher of the gospel for your particular time in your unique place? What is God calling you to do?

3. In your parish, what are your strongest memories of solidarity? What are moments that have divided you? How can you strengthen that sense of solidarity?

4. What good things are already happening in the conversation between pulpit and pew in your parish? How can you build those up?

5. If "we are all in this together" to help each other flourish, what support can you offer to some person who ministers to you? Could you send a note, a comment, a "keep it up," or give an expression of thanks?

9 Preaching as an Act of Love within a Milieu of Caring

1. What is one thing that can you do today to give support, provide feedback, or offer encouragement to the homilist that you heard last Sunday? If you were the homilist, what is one thing that you could do to seek support, feedback, or encouragement?

2. Listening skills are necessary for effective communication in any situation, whether in a parish discussion group, a parent–child interaction, talking with an atheist, a counseling session or when giving the sacraments to the dying. Do you know someone who is a really good listener? What does that person do or say? What is one thing that person does that you would like to imitate?

3. As you share, offer specifics about the content of the homily: What do you not understand about your faith? What do you not know that you do not understand? What would help you to understand? The style of the homily: how do you learn best—stories, explanations, examples, exhortation, prayerfulness, allusions to music or art, tying a message in with a movie or TV show? What helps you to grow in faith?

4. What are your hopes for the future of the homily? If the Sunday preaching were the very best that it could be, what would that look like? How would it impact you, your family and friends?

5. If you as pulpit and pew are reading this together, what is one thing that you as a parish can do differently as a result of this discussion?

For Private Reflection (or with one trusted other, a friend or spiritual director)

1. The healing of memories: Make a list of the times that someone in the church has hurt you. List the times that someone in the church has blessed you. Which list is longer? Write next to those painful memories, "I forgive you"; next to the blessed memories, "I thank you." (What is the reason for the tradition of "counting your blessings" at the end of the day? The positives are often harder to recall than the negatives.) Take that list to prayer daily, continue to give forgiveness, and ask for healing. Or find someone you trust and pray about this together.

2. What do you do when someone is spewing negativities about the church, a parish, or a preacher? (for discussion groups, evangelization visitations, friend interchanges, family meals, or other)

   • Give them a moment to vent (not 25 minutes); to describe their feelings; ask careful clarifying questions so that you understand what they are talking about.

   • Affirm their feelings by saying, "that must have been painful for you (hurtful, difficult, made you angry)."

- If they are at a place where you can ask this, gently inquire, "Do you have any warm memories of . . . (fill in the blank of: preacher, parish, church, God, as needed)?" or "Can you tell me about . . . (something positive that you may have picked up in the conversation)?" or "I can see how you would feel that way. What about seeing it this way . . . (tell the story from a different perspective)?" Seek out any points of positive connection; don't fall into complaining together; that reinforces the negative stories that are running in their head.

- Thus, seek to tie in and then gently stretch, working to recast that negative memory toward a more positive one. Keep listening. Healing can be a slow process, or it can come from an "aha!" moment. Ask the Holy Spirit who is the Healer to work within them.

For Further Prayer, Reflection, and Study

1. As you gather together to pray and study the Scriptures for the upcoming Sunday, ask yourselves these questions:

   - What are the connection points between this Scripture passage and the everyday lives of the people who will be listening?

   - What is top-of-the-mind for the listeners on this Sunday? To what needs will you be preaching? Where would they like to grow in faith?

   - What interests/perspectives/worries/concerns/struggles do you have in common with them?

   - What message does the gospel provide for those concerns?

2. As this book draws to a close, you may wonder, where do we go from here? If you've read this book as a study group, here are some suggestions about where you can go from here (some are explicitly Catholic books, others are not):

   - To form a preaching preparation team: read *Fulfilled in Your Hearing* together. It has suggestions for how to run a preparation group.

   - A group of clergy could study: *Preaching Better* by Ken Untener or *We Speak the Word of the Lord: A Practical Plan for More Effective Preaching* by Daniel Harris; *Made to Stick: Why Some Ideas Survive and Others Die* by Chip and Dan Heath; plus the above.

- Clergy with parish or diocesan staff: *Difficult Conversations: How to Discuss What Matters Most,* by Stone, Patton, and Heen; if you are all tired, *The Fully Alive Preacher: Recovering from Homiletical Burn-out,* Mike Graves; plus all of the above.

- Parish study groups: *Difficult Conversations: How to Discuss What Matters Most,* by Stone, Patton, and Heen; any of the above.

- If you are all alone, read: *Difficult Conversations: How to Discuss What Matters Most,* by Stone, Patton, and Heen; or *Switch: How to Change Things When Change Is Hard;* there are many good books on developing your own spirituality in spite of what is happening around you; my personal favorites are: *The Practice of the Presence of God* by Brother Lawrence, *The Philokalia* (anthology in four volumes), and *Speak Lord, Your Servant is Listening* by David E. Rosage (going out of print, but worth reprinting), plus many books of the saints and other spiritual reading.

- As this book goes to press, Pope Francis has published his apostolic exhortation, *Evangelii Gaudium.* Chapter 3, The Proclamation of the Gospel, is a rich source of insight for a preaching study group.

Notes

Chapter 1—pages 1–11

1. The names of people and schools and parishes have been changed to protect the anonymity of the respondents. In addition, none of the interviews or surveys (and only one of the stories) came from my own parish, so my friends and clergy and parish community are off the hook. They have prayed for me and this project, and I am deeply grateful.

2. Karla Bellinger, "Are You Talking to Me? A Study of Young Listeners' Connection with Catholic Sunday Preaching" (DMin diss., Aquinas Institute of Theology, 2012), some of which is available online: http://www.thecenterforpep.com /our-work/research-initiatives/are-you-talking-to-me-a-study-of-young -listeners-connection-with-sunday-preaching.

3. The *Catechesis in Preaching Initiative* was a collaboration between the National Conference for Catechetical Leadership and the Center for Preaching, Evangelization, and Prayer in May–July 2013. The complete research report is online: http://www.thecenterforpep.com/our-work/research-initiatives /the-catechesis-in-preaching-initiative/.

4. Donald R. McCrabb, "Improving Preaching through Feedback," *Seminary Journal* 16, no. 2 (Fall 2010): 5–6.

5. Lori Carrell, *The Great American Sermon Survey* (Wheaton, IL: Mainstay Church Resources, 2000), 95.

6. It is a popular misconception that we are awash in studies about preaching. There are very few.

7. The insights of the Harvard Negotiation Project are described in Douglas Stone, Bruce Patton, and Sheila Heen, *Difficult Conversations: How to Discuss What Matters Most* (New York: Penguin, 1999).

8. Benedict XVI, *Verbum Domini* (Post-Synodal Apostolic Exhortation on the Word of God, 2010), no. 59.

9. United States Conference of Catholic Bishops, *Preaching the Mystery of Faith: The Sunday Homily* (Washington, DC: United States Conference of Catholic Bishops, 2012), 17.

10. Daniel E. Harris, *We Speak the Word of the Lord: A Practical Plan for More Effective Preaching* (Skokie, IL: ACTA Publications, 2001), 24.

11. A nationally representative study of preaching is suggested among the research recommendations in chapter 9.

12. Though originating from a Catholic context, much of the material in this book can be modified for Protestant and Orthodox situations as well. The discussion questions can also be adapted.

Chapter 2—pages 12–30

1. Benedict XVI, *Porta Fidei* (Apostolic Letter for the Indiction of the Year of Faith, 2011), no. 2. See also Karla J. Bellinger, "My Heart Burns Within Me: Sunday Preaching and the Catechesis of Young People," *Catechetical Leader* 24, no. 3 (May 2013): 20–23.

2. Pew Research Religion and Public Life Project, "'Nones' on the Rise," October 9, 2012, http://www.pewforum.org/2012/10/09/nones-on-the-rise.

3. John Paul II, Opening Address of the Nineteenth General Assembly of CELAM, March 9, 1983, Port-au-Prince, Haiti, in *L'Osservatore Romano,* English Edition 16/780 (April 18, 1983): 9.

4. United States Conference of Catholic Bishops, *Preaching the Mystery of Faith* (Washington, DC: United States Conference of Catholic Bishops, 2012).

5. Chip Heath and Dan Heath, *Made to Stick: Why Some Ideas Survive and Others Die*, 2nd ed. (New York: Random House, 2008), 20.

6. As a result of this understanding, I have made an attempt to use the non-technical language of everyday use wherever possible in this book.

7. Congregation for the Doctrine of the Faith, *Doctrinal Note on Some Aspects of Evangelization* (2007), 8.

8. These three target populations for the new evangelization were clearly delineated in Pope Benedict XVI's homily for the closing Mass of the Synod of Bishops on the New Evangelization, October 28, 2012, found at http://www.vatican.va/holy_father/benedict_xvi/homilies/2012/documents/hf_ben-xvi_hom_20121028_conclusione-sinodo_en.html.

9. The data that is quoted in this book comes from my doctoral thesis, *Are You Talking to Me? A Study of Young Listeners' Connection with Catholic Sunday Preaching*, Aquinas Institute, May 2012. Lamenting the lack of empirical studies in preaching, Andrew Greeley has stated that about one in five (20 percent) Catholics report that the homilies that they hear are excellent. See Greeley, "A Catholic Revival?" *America* (April 10, 1999), 8–14. This current empirical data comes from the population of Catholic high school students who attended Mass at least once per month; their one of six "yes, I would recommend" was slightly lower than Greeley's estimate, but approximately in the same range.

10. Center for Applied Research in the Apostolate (CARA), "Sacraments Today: Belief and Practice Among U.S. Catholics," http://www.cara.georgetown .edu/sacramentsreport.pdf, 7.

11. Ibid., 54.

12. Ibid., 7.

13. About a third (32 percent) of high school Mass-attending students in my study said that the reason that they came was "I was required to." Those who said that they came "to worship God" were 41.3 percent, the highest of the responses. A few gave more than one reason. *Are You Talking to Me?*, q. 37.

14. CARA, "A Micro-scoping View of U.S. Catholic Populations," http:// nineteensixty-four.blogspot.com/2012/05/microscoping-view-of-us-catholic .html.

15. Ibid.

16. Ken Untener, *Preaching Better: Practical Suggestions for Homilists* (Mahwah, NJ: Paulist Press, 1999), 101.

17. Christian Smith, *Soul Searching: The Religious and Spiritual Lives of American Teenagers* (New York: Oxford University Press, 2005), 28.

18. The Bishops Committee on Priestly Life and Ministry, *Fulfilled in Your Hearing: The Homily in the Sunday Assembly* (Washington, DC: United States Catholic Conference, 1982), 2.

19. *Preaching the Mystery of Faith,* 5.

20. *Are You Talking to Me?,* 161.

21. Ibid., 156.

22. Katherine Schmitt, "Effective Preaching: What Catholics Want—A Project of the NCEA Seminary Department," *Seminary Journal* 16, no. 2 (Fall 2010): 26.

23. Pope Francis, Homily for the Chrism Mass (Saint Peter's Basilica, March 28, 2013), http://www.vatican.va/holy_father/francesco/homilies/2013/documents/ papa-francesco_20130328_messa-crismale_en.html.

24. Malcolm Gladwell, *The Tipping Point: How Little Things Can Make a Big Difference* (New York: Little, Brown, 2002), 99–102.

25. Benedict XVI, *Ubicumque et Semper,* (Motu Proprio establishing the Pontifical Council for Promoting the New Evangelization, 2010), http:// www.vatican.va/holy_father/benedict_xvi/apost_letters/documents/hf _ben-xvi_apl_20100921_ubicumque-et-semper_en.html.

26. Interestingly, their opinion of the quality of the homily did not correlate with the reason that they came to Mass; those whose parents required them to be there had equally positive and negative experiences of preaching. Hence the lesson for parents is not to stop requiring Mass attendance but to seek for those experiences to be as positive as possible. But that is another book entirely.

27. *Are You Talking to Me?* qq. 26–35.

28. Wayne D. Hoyer and Deborah J. MacInnis, *Consumer Behavior,* 3rd ed. (Boston: Houghton Mifflin, 2008), 291.

29. Ibid.

30. American Religious Identification Survey 2008, "American Nones: The Profile of the No Religion Population," http://commons.trincoll.edu/aris /files/2011/08/NONES_08.pdf, 2.

31. CARA, 54; Pew Research Religion and Public Life Project, "The Catholic 'Swing' Vote," October 11, 2012, http://www.pewforum.org/2012/10/11 /the-catholic-swing-vote/.

32. CARA, Sacraments, 40.

33. Hoyer and MacInnis, 281.

34. CARA, Sacraments, 56.

35. See Karla J. Bellinger, "Vatican II: Connecting with the Next Generation," *AIM: Liturgy Resources* (Aug–Nov 2013).

36. CARA, Sacraments, 20. This increased by 7 percent between 2002 and 2008.

37. *Are You Talking to Me?,* question 84.

38. Many had more than one thing to say about why they don't attend Mass. Responses were categorized and then measured.

39. For valuable insight into preaching at funerals, see James Wallace, *Preaching to the Hungers of the Heart: The Homily on the Feasts and within the Rites* (Collegeville, MN: Liturgical Press, 2002).

40. Mass attendance is often measured from among those who self-identify. Since my survey was taken by entire theology classes, it asked about baptism and attendance, which may result in responses that differ from those studies that evaluate self-identified Catholics. Approximately 10 percent of those "raised Catholic" as defined by up to their sixteenth birthday have left the faith of their upbringing (Pew Religious Landscape). The fourteen-year-olds from my study who have already walked away from their faith thus would not be included in that population of self-identified Catholics. Yet the responses of young formerly Catholic teens can also be instructive.

41. Pew, "'Nones' on the Rise."

42. Ibid.: "The vast majority of religiously unaffiliated Americans are not actively seeking to find a church or other religious group to join. Leaving aside atheists or agnostics, just 10% of those who describe their current religion as 'nothing in particular' say they are looking for a religion that is right for them; 88% say they are not."

43. Ibid.

44. Al Ries and Jack Trout, *Positioning: The Battle for your Mind: How to be Seen and Heard in the Overcrowded Marketplace* (New York: McGraw-Hill, 2001), 7.

45. For a social commentary on how much more alone we are in this connected world, see Charlene deGuzman and Miles Crawford, "I Forgot My Phone,"

YouTube video, 2:10, posted by "charstarleneTV," August 22, 2013, http://www
.youtube.com/watch?v=OINa46HeWg8.

46. Sociable Labs, "Social Impact: How Consumers See It," http://www
.sociablelabs.com//Social-Impact-Study-2012.

Chapter 3—pages 31–42

1. Occasionally, kids have no adult to turn to. When asked to describe "who
connects with you," sixteen young people (3 percent) answered "No one": "There
are no adults that really 'connect' with me." Only one student suggested that connecting with adults was hopeless: "No matter how hard they try to connect with
us, it just won't work. We connect better with people our own age."

2. Interestingly, when experts express (minor) doubts, they are more readily
believed. Uma R. Karmarkar and Zakary L. Tormala, "Believe Me, I Have No
Idea What I'm Talking About: The Effects of Source Certainty on Consumer In-
volvement and Persuasion," *Journal of Consumer Research* 36, no. 6 (2010): 1033–42.

3. Clergy and hospital chaplains often establish this type of tie with people whom
they have visited in the hospital or whose loved one they have anointed before death.

4. Karla J. Bellinger, "Ten Ways to Make Human Connections with Today's
Catholic Youth" (presentation, NCEA National Convention, Houston, TX, 2013).

5. Jerome Murphy-O'Connor, *Paul: A Critical Life* (New York: Oxford University Press, 1996), 322.

6. See chapter 4 in "The Church as Sacrament" in Avery Dulles, *Models of
the Church* (New York: Random House, 2000).

7. Bruce J. Malina, *The New Testament World: Insights from Cultural Anthropology*,
3rd ed. (Louisville: Westminster John Knox, 2001), 61.

8. Pope John XXIII, "Address on the occasion of the solemn opening of the
Most Holy Council" (October 11, 1962), http://www.vatican.va/holy_father
/john_xxiii/speeches/1962/index_en.htm.

9. Avery Dulles, "Vatican II: The Myth and the Reality," *America*, February
24, 2003, 7–11. Dulles asked who could have foreseen the fifty-year tug and pull
since the Council between preserving the continuity of received truth on the one
hand and the challenge of putting it into the words of the people on the other?

10. Louis-Marie Chauvet, *The Sacraments: The Word of God at the Mercy of the
Body* (Collegeville, MN: Liturgical Press, 2001), 36–37.

11. Second Vatican Council, *Sacrosanctum Concilium* (Constitution on the
Sacred Liturgy, 1963), 56.

12. Daniel E. Harris, *We Speak the Word of the Lord: A Practical Plan for More
Effective Preaching* (Skokie, IL: ACTA Publications, 2001), 24.

13. Committee on Priestly Life and Ministry, *Fulfilled in Your Hearing: The Homily
in the Sunday Assembly* (Washington, DC: United States Catholic Conference, 1982).

Chapter 4—pages 45–59

1. Otis Carl Edwards, Jr., *A History of Preaching* (Nashville: Abingdon, 2004), 9.

2. Ibid., 40.

3. Ibid., 34.

4. And is still in use by many Christian congregations.

5. John Chrysostom, *On the Priesthood*, 5, in Philip Schaff, *Nicene and Post-Nicene Fathers* I.9 (Grand Rapids, MI: Christian Classics Ethereal Library), http://www.ccel.org/ccel/schaff/npnf109.html.

6. Edwards, 112.

7. The fifteen sermons attributed to St. Boniface in the eighth century were largely catechetical instructions.

8. Hughes Oliphant Old, *The Reading and Preaching of the Scriptures in the Worship of the Christian Church: the Medieval Period* (Grand Rapids, MI: Wm. B. Eerdmans, 1999), 198.

9. Deborah Youngs, *The Life-Cycle in Western Europe, c. 1300–1500* (New York: Palgrave, 2006), 29.

10. Josef Jungmann, SJ, "The Defeat of Teutonic Arianism and the Revolution in Religious Culture in the Early Middle Ages," in *Pastoral Liturgy* (New York: Herder & Herder, 1962), 66.

11. Ibid., 69, 79.

12. Germany produced an unprecedented outpouring of pamphlets, perhaps 300,000 copies of Luther's writings between 1517 and 1520. Literacy rates in northern European countries grew faster than in the south. See R. A. Houston, "Literacy," *Encyclopedia of European Social History,* ed. Peter Stearns (Detroit: Charles Scribner's Sons, 2001), 5:391–406.

13. Stephen DeLeers, *Written Text Becomes Living Word: The Vision and Practice of Sunday Preaching* (Collegeville, MN: Liturgical Press, 2004), 3.

14. Thomas Bokenkotter, *A Concise History of the Catholic Church* (New York: Doubleday, 1990), 226.

15. Hubert Jedin, *A History of the Council of Trent,* Vol. 1 (London: Thomas Nelson and Sons, 1957), 165.

16. DeLeers, 3.

17. Edwards, 275, citing Baintain's *Erasmus,* 268.

18. Ibid., 338, 341.

19. Ibid., 334, quoting Council of Trent, Fifth Session, "Decree on Reformation," ch. 2.

20. Conversely, focus on the sacraments, sacramentals, and the contemplative dimensions of spirituality were considered "too Catholic" by many Protestants.

21. Old, 160.

22. Pius X, On the French Law of Separation (*Vehementer Nos*), February 11, 1906, 8.

23. A fine example of this was Jacques-Marie-Louis Monsabré. This popular French Dominican preached Catholic belief in his Sunday homilies for seventeen years. When all of his transcribed homilies were compiled into a 48-volume work, he had systematically covered the entirety of Christian doctrine.

24. Pius X, *The 1917 Pio-Benedictine Code of Canon Law: In English Translation* (San Francisco: Ignatius, 2001), 453.

25. Trivia Library, "A History of Advertising in America in the 1930's and 1940's," http://www. trivia-library.com/a/history-of-advertising-in-america -in-the-1930s-and-1940s.htm.

26. O'Brien Atkinson, *How to Make Us Want Your Sermon: By a Listener* (New York: Joseph F. Wagner, Inc., 1942).

27. Ibid., v.

28. Ibid., ix.

29. Ibid., x. The median number of years of schooling in the United States in 1940 was 8.4 years. Clergy were among the educated elite; Catholics tended to be less educated than average; immigrants from southern and eastern European countries were poorly educated at that time. As a result of this dichotomy, there was great respect for men of the cloth as authorities "up there." See http://www .census.gov/population/socdemo/education/p10-8/p10-8.pdf.

30. Ibid., 5.

31. A professor during my time there said, "If only we could get as much buzz for Jesus as we get for the football team. . . ."

32. The original story of Pentecost is a prime example of "buzz"—we in the church know that inner motivation when we see it; hopefully, we have experienced it. A gut-level reaction may be to dismiss this secular body of information, as though we in the church are "above" it, as we were once indifferent to the Protestant reformers' preaching. But at what cost? A search for understanding here could bear much fruit.

33. Shea found a consistently high level of perceived disrespect among both the adult and teen listeners that he surveyed. This mindset may be a contributing factor to that perception, asking, "Does it matter to you that *I* am here?" See David J. Shea, "Unmet Needs in Catholic Preaching: A Project of the Archdiocese of Cincinnati," *Seminary Journal* 16, no. 2 (Fall 2010): 33–42.

34. To understand these methods of persuasion more fully, see "The Persuaders" from PBS at http://www.pbs.org/wgbh/pages/frontline/shows/persuaders/.

35. The practical application: don't make the sign of the cross before or after the homily, since that implies that it is distinct from the liturgical action.

36. DeLeers, 13. For a thorough analysis of the evolution of the documents about preaching from 1963–1993, see DeLeers' second chapter.

37. Second Vatican Council, *Apostolicam Actuositatem* (Decree on the Apostolate of Lay People, 1965), no. 2.

38. Paul VI, *Evangelii Nuntiandi* (Apostolic Letter on Evangelization in the Modern World, 1975), no. 43.

Chapter 5—pages 60–77

1. Part of the detective work for my doctoral thesis was to ask parish priests what "connection" means to them as the men "in the trenches." The homiletics world has not often heard the voices of those who preach day to day, to ask what the strengths and struggles of preaching are for them. The comments in this chapter come from the transcriptions of those interviews, as well as from other informal conversations with clergy.

2. Timothy Dolan, *Priests for the Third Millennium* (Huntington, IN: Our Sunday Visitor, 2000), 229.

3. United States Conference of Catholic Bishops, *Preaching the Mystery of Faith*, (Washington, DC: United States Conference of Catholic Bishops, 2012), 34–40.

4. Second Vatican Council, *Presbyterorum Ordinis* (Decree on the Ministry and Life of Priests, 1965), no. 4.

5. Priestly identity was strongly emphasized beginning with the 1993 edition of *The Program for Priestly Formation*; now in its fifth edition; portions on identity are now nos. 25, 198–200.

6. Pew Forum on Religion and Public Life, "Catholics Share Bishops Concerns about Religious Liberty," November 2012, http://www.pewforum.org /Politics-and-Elections/Catholics-Share-Bishops-Concerns-about-Religious -Liberty.aspx#leaders.

7. Portions of this section originally appeared in Karla J. Bellinger, "My Heart Burns within Me: Sunday Preaching and the Catechesis of Young People," *Catechetical Leader* 24, no. 3 (May 2013): 20–23.

8. Joseph Kurtz (Archbishop of Louisville) in discussion with the author, September 2012, and email message to author, February 7, 2013.

9. Andre Resner, "Ethos," *The New Interpreter's Handbook of Preaching*, ed. Paul Scott Wilson et al. (Nashville: Abingdon, 2008), 350.

10. Katherine Schmitt, "Effective Preaching: What Catholics Want—A Project of the NCEA Seminary Department," *Seminary Journal* 16, no. 2 (Fall 2010): 26.

11. John Paul II, *Pastores Dabo Vobis* (Post-Synodal Apostolic Exhortation on the Formation of Priests, 1992), no. 73.

12. United States Conference of Catholic Bishops, *The Basic Plan for Ongoing Formation of Clergy*, 7. The unifying thread . . . is the grace and the task of *integration*, which fosters the living synthesis of priestly identity and priestly service.

13. *Preaching the Mystery of Faith,* 46.

14. With the shortage of priests, the amount of time spent as a parochial vicar has also shortened. Men become pastors more quickly after ordination. One priest friend of mine has been ordained seven years and now is pastor of two parishes, the diocesan vocations director, and chaplain to a Catholic high school. I jokingly asked him, "When are they going to make you bishop to lighten your load?" One way to make a good man ineffective is to give him so much to do that he cannot do any of it well.

15. For more on the demographics of the priesthood, see Mary Gautier, Paul M. Perl, and Stephen J. Fichter, *Same Call, Different Men: The Evolution of the Priesthood since Vatican II* (Collegeville, MN: Liturgical Press, 2012), 1–17.

16. Ibid., 18–47. For refreshment in preaching, see Mike Grave, *The Fully Alive Preacher: Recovering from Homiletical Burnout* (Louisville: Westminster John Knox, 2006). Though not from a Catholic author, its concrete suggestions nonetheless will enhance the creativity and vitality of exhausted preaching.

17. Rick Sterns, personal communication, December 1, 2011, says that informal surveys of entering homiletic students have consistently demonstrated that about 15 percent of those coming into the priesthood report doing so because they want to preach. Ironically, this is the same percentage of homilies that young people would recommend to a friend.

18. CARA, "Priests in the United States: Satisfaction, Work Load and Support Structures," CARA Working Paper No. 5, Center for Applied Research in the Apostolate, Georgetown University, 2002. http://www.stmsfc.org/WORK LOADFORPRIESTS%201%2024%2010.pdf.

19. Lori J. Carrell, *The Great American Sermon Survey* (Wheaton, IL: Mainstay Church Resources, 2000), 119, 139.

20. O'Brien Atkinson, *How to Make Us Want Your Sermon: By a Listener* (New York: Joseph F. Wagner, 1942), 137.

21. *National Council of Catholic Bishops, Renewing the Vision: A Framework for Catholic Youth Ministry* (Washington, DC: United States Conference of Catholic Bishops, 1997).

22. National Initiative for Adolescent Catechesis (NIAC) at http://adolescent catechesis.org/.

23. Congregation for the Clergy, *General Directory for Catechesis*, nos. 260 and 57. http://www.vatican.va/roman_curia/congregations/cclergy/documents /rc_con_ccatheduc_doc_17041998_directory-for-catechesis_en.html.

24. David Shea, "Unmet Needs in Catholic Preaching: A Project of the Arch-diocese of Cincinnati," *Seminary Journal* 16 (2010): 33.

25. There is a remarkable consistency: Peter Lovrick, "A Pedagogical Model for Homiletics at St. Augustine's Seminary: They Must Increase, and I Must Decrease," DMin thesis, Aquinas Institute, 2009, 35, where 81.8 percent of those in the Toronto archdiocese considered themselves good to excellent; and David J. Shea, "Self-Understanding in Catholic Preaching: How the Identity of the Priest Shapes his Approach to Preaching," DMin thesis, Aquinas Institute, 2006, 72, where 82 percent in his Cincinnati archdiocese considered themselves above average or better.

26. Shea, "Self-Understanding in Catholic Preaching," 98.

27. Lovrick, 36. These findings directly correspond with what laypeople have said in both my survey and in David Shea's survey.

28. Lovrick, 173.

29. If you are reading this book, thank you.

30. Lovrick, 41.

31. Carrell, 147.

32. Ibid., 133, 137. Often, feedback from one vocal listener can impact the direction that the preacher takes in his homilies even though it may not represent the broader listening population.

33. A few deacons may though. . . . Hearing that earlier interchange might enlighten a preacher as to why that thirteen-year-old in the second pew has his arms crossed, his legs splayed out, and that frown on his face. It may have nothing whatsoever to do with the homily.

34. Wayne D. Hoyer and Deborah J. MacInnis, *Consumer Behavior,* 3rd ed. (Boston: Houghton Mifflin, 2008), 398.

35. Manuel Flores, SJ, "Lessons from Evangelicals" *America* (July 19, 2004).

36. For an in-depth analysis of trends in seminaries, see Katarina Schuth, *Theologates Seminaries, Theologates, and the Future of Church Ministry: An Analysis of Trends and Transitions* (Collegeville, MN: Liturgical Press, 1999).

37. Richard Stern, unpublished essay shared with the author, July 26, 2010.

38. A deeper level of research is needed to broaden the picture of clergy concerns in relation to preaching improvement. This small sample of interviews focused on the struggles of individual preachers. To get a fuller picture of cultural obstacles, other questions beg to be asked. These are beyond the scope of this project, but opening the conversation would provide additional insights.

39. Pope Francis, "A Big Heart Open to God," interview with Antonio Spadaro, SJ, in *America* (September 30, 2013).

40. *The Basic Plan for Ongoing Formation of Clergy,* 7.

41. *Presbyterorum Ordinis,* 2.

Chapter 6—pages 78–91

1. Ken Untener, *Preaching Better: Practical Suggestions for Homilists* (Mahwah, NJ: Paulist, 1999), 1.

2. David J. Shea, "Unmet Needs in Catholic Preaching: A Project of the Archdiocese of Cincinnati," *Seminary Journal* 16, no. 2 (Fall 2010), 40. For a stellar set of articles on preaching, see the entire *Seminary Journal's* Fall 2010 issue.

3. For a description of that process, see http://www.thecenterforpep.com /our-work.

4. Both Shea and Untener discovered this: laypeople's hopes were higher than they (and by implication, most other Catholic preachers) had previously thought.

5. Your answer may depend on where you get your sources of information. For a fun read, see Rolf Dobelli, "Why You Shouldn't Read the News: News Illusion," chap. 99 in *The Art of Thinking Clearly* (New York: HarperCollins, 2013), 296–98. People who rely heavily on the news/social media/television, etc., statistically have a more negative view of life than those who look around them. Also see: W. M. Johnston and G. C. L. Davey, "The psychological impact of negative TV news bulletins: The catastrophizing of personal worries," *British Journal of Psychology* 88 (1997): 85–91.

6. Pope Paul VI, *Apostolicam Actuositatem* (Decree on the Apostolate of the Laity, November 18, 1965), no. 5, http://www.vatican.va/archive/hist_councils /ii_vatican_council/documents/vat-ii_decree_19651118_apostolicam -actuositatem_en.html.

7. As translated into English at http://www.lifeteen.com/blog/vigil -homily-by-pope-benedict-at-world-youth-day-2011.

8. http://wesley.nnu.edu/john-wesley/the-sermons-of-john-wesley -1872-edition/sermon-2-the-almost-christian.

9. This number is based on the assumption that the average number of words per song is 30; therefore the 40,000 songs that the recorder holds results in 1,200,000 words.

10. http://www.law.nyu.edu/about/sustainability/whatyoucando/junkmail.

11. http://www.perimetec.com/7-Things-You-Didnt-Know-About-Email -Spam-Worldwide.php.

12. Al Ries and Jack Trout, *Positioning: The Battle for Your Mind: How to be Seen and Heard in the Overcrowded Marketplace* (New York: McGraw-Hill, 2001), 7.

13. Chip Heath and Dan Heath, *Made to Stick: Why Some Ideas Survive and Others Die*, 2nd ed. (New York: Random House, 2008), 20.

14. Smith characterizes this contemporary mindset as "Moralistic Therapeutic Deism"—God wants people to be nice, good, and fair, a divine butler who will come running when you need him; the central goal of life is to be happy and to feel good about oneself; that nice people all go to heaven. See Christian Smith,

Soul Searching: The Religious and Spiritual Lives of American Teenagers (New York: Oxford University Press, 2005), 162–71.

15. For a deeper analysis of this cultural perspective, see the Karla J. Bellinger, "To Be Young and Catholic in the U.S." in *Momentum* (March 2014).

16. Malcolm Gladwell, *The Tipping Point: How Little Things Can Make a Big Difference* (New York: Little, Brown, 2002), 99–102.

17. "Interesting Fact: There's a Yawning Need for Boring Professors," *The Wall Street Journal*, Feb. 25, 2013, http://online.wsj.com/news/articles/SB100014241 27887323864304578316162117673132.

18. Wayne D. Hoyer and Deborah J. MacInnis, *Consumer Behavior*, 3rd ed. (Boston: Houghton Mifflin, 2008), 116–27.

19. Gail Ramshaw, *Reviving Sacred Speech: The Meaning of Liturgical Language* (Akron, OH: OSL Publications, 2000), 25.

20. Hoyer and MacInnis, 84.

21. Heath and Heath, 65.

22. Hoyer and MacInnis, 91. "Habituation" is the reason that stimuli pass into the background and we no longer pay attention to them.

23. Ibid., 95. In "pre-attentive processing," we pay just enough attention to know that it is going on.

24. Ibid., 60.

25. Robert B. Cialdini, *Influence: The Psychology of Persuasion* (New York: Harper Collins, 2007), 173. This factor is often used in youth ministry in peer-led retreats for this very reason. The faith of one young person can be very influential in impacting the faith of another.

26. Interview with Clifford Nass, "Multitasking May Not Mean Higher Productivity," August 28, 2009; http://www.npr.org/templates/story/story .php?storyId=112334449.

27. Hoyer and MacInnis, 84.

28. The first workshop of the CONNECT process for youth and clergy focuses on strengthening listening skills as the two groups begin to work together to listen to God (in *lectio divina*) and to each other in preparing homilies that connect pulpit and pew. When they help to craft the message, listeners are also more engaged in that message.

29. Untener, 101.

30. Hoyer and MacInnis, 84.

31. http://www.gallup.com/poll/154169/Chronic-Pain-Rates-Shoot-Until -Americans-Reach-Late-50s.aspx?ref=image.

32. For more on this, see Karla J. Bellinger, "To Be Young and Catholic in the U.S."

33. An interesting experiment is for a listener to write down all of the thoughts that came into his or her head while someone else is speaking. Awareness of the factors of attention actually helps to focus attention.

34. From Shea's article in the *Seminary Journal*, at least 50 percent of parishioners would be happy if they got that much.

35. For an in-depth look at homiletical evaluations and their implicitly theological implications, see Karla J. Bellinger, "And . . . How's It Going? Preaching Itself as Difficult Conversation," presented at the Academy of Homiletics, December 2013, in Louisville, KY.

36. Multiplied by the four years that the seminarian spent in high school listening to preaching that went over his head—that totals 1,664 minutes of wasted opportunity.

37. Though not always. You have to learn the culture of your people to read bodily feedback accurately. Some people listen best with their eyes closed. Some simply do not respond physically, but may be totally "with you." One preacher told me that he was very discouraged by the lack of response until he did a survey. It turned out that his "unresponsive" people were getting a lot from his preaching.

38. Many thanks to Dr. William Baker for this and many other insights during our "Marketing and Preaching" independent study course at the University of Akron.

39. Heath and Heath, 177.

40. Hoyer and MacInnis, 55–58.

41. United States Conference of Catholic Bishops, *Preaching the Mystery of Faith: the Sunday Homily* (Washington, DC: United States Conference of Catholic Bishops, 2012), 9.

Chapter 7—pages 92–112

1. This young man of sixteen represents the average age at which the ordained class of 2011 decided to enter the priesthood. See: Center for Applied Research in the Apostolate (CARA), "The Class of 2011: Survey of Ordinands to the Priesthood," CARA, http://www.usccb.org/beliefs-and-teachings/vocations/ordination-class/upload/ordination-class-2011-report.pdf.

2. Group I—baptized Catholics who attended Mass at least once per month; Group II—baptized Catholics who were not attending Mass regularly; Group III—non-baptized Catholics whose experience of preaching at Mass came from their Catholic school experience. In Group III, when divided into Protestants who attend services regularly and those who are "nones," the frustration with Catholic preaching was higher among those who go to church regularly elsewhere. (That would also make for an interesting population to study further.)

3. That is a good thing—many preachers work hard not to be judgmental in their preaching. The ideal would be for harsh/judgmental to be zero (0 percent)—even the one of twelve to fifteen who checked this as their experience is too high, given the level of authority of the man who preaches and the location from which he speaks.

4. This is a topic that begs further research to uncover what the homily has to do with why they are not there.

5. For a detailed literature review of the marginalization of youth in preaching (and not just in Catholic preaching), see Richard W. Voelz, "Preaching, Adolescent Youth, and the Turn to the 'Other': An Agenda for Homiletics," paper presented at the Academy of Homiletics, Minneapolis, MN, December 2007.

6. From his study with adults, Shea says, "More than half cite the homily content issues not being relevant to daily life/today's world, unfocused/not on a single topic, not connecting to today's readings, and simply being too boring or repetitious. David J. Shea, "Unmet Needs in Catholic Preaching: A Project of the Archdiocese of Cincinnati," *Seminary Journal* 16, no. 2 (Fall 2010), 35.

7. Ken Untener, *Preaching Better: Practical Suggestions for Homilists* (Mahwah, NJ: Paulist, 1999), 5.

8. Except for the two schools that required permission slips. Some kids forgot.

9. These ten descriptors were originally created from the listener responses that were later reported in Katherine Schmitt, "Effective Preaching: What Catholics Want—A Project of the NCEA Seminary Department," *Seminary Journal* 16 (2010), 26–30; they were then adapted to accord with early focus group responses.

10. Al Ries and Jack Trout, *Positioning: The Battle for Your Mind: How to be Seen and Heard in the Overcrowded Marketplace* (New York: McGraw-Hill, 2001), 18.

11. Chip Heath and Dan Heath, *Made to Stick: Why Some Ideas Survive and Others Die*, 2nd ed. (New York: Random House, 2008), 37.

12. Wayne D. Hoyer and Deborah J. MacInnis, *Consumer Behavior*, 3rd ed. (Boston: Houghton Mifflin, 2008), 135.

13. The question about growth in faith built off of the previous question of sixteen characteristics. The follow-up question asked: "If you marked the box above 'helped me grow in my faith' or 'uplifting, made me a better person,' what was that experience like? Please describe that as clearly as you can." When these qualitative responses were categorized, they revealed clear fruits of discipleship growth.

14. Mary Alice Mulligan, Diane-Turner-Sharazz, Dawn Ottoni Wilhelm, and Ronald J. Allen, the authors of *Believing in Preaching: What Listeners Hear in Sermons* (St. Louis: Chalice Press, 2005) categorize listeners' responses of what God is actively doing in a sermon into four groupings: God acts in providing the specific message; God is active in inspiring the construction of the sermon; God is active

in actually performing tasks in the congregation; and God is active in assisting the listeners (pp.152–53). This young lady's comment fits best in this last grouping.

15. This primacy of "understanding" as the most prominent long-term response parallels Lori Carrell's experience that 95 percent of the sermons that she evaluates *inform rather than transform*. See Lori J. Carrell, *Preaching that Matters: Reflective Practices for Transforming Sermons* (Herndon, VA: The Alban Institute, 2013), 45. It also reinforces Reid's plea that learning-centered sermons shift from information toward spiritual formation in the Protestant tradition. See Robert Stephen Reid, "Learning-Centered Preaching for Practice-Centered Congregations," paper presented at the Academy of Homiletics, Austin, TX, 2011.

16. Delivery problems: Similar to the one of three delivery issues that this study found, in Shea's work with adults, three of ten mentioned: using a monotone voice, reading the homily, poor enunciation, not connecting with the congregation, and using a condescending tone. See Shea, 36.

17. Daniel E. Harris, *We Speak the Word of the Lord: A Practical Plan for More Effective Preaching* (Skokie, IL: ACTA, 2001), 24.

18. Robert J. McCarty, "Young People are Listening! Preaching and Liturgy with Youth," *Seminary Journal* 13, no. 2 (2007), 27.

Part Three—pages 113–14

1. Karl Rahner, *Foundations of Christian Faith: An Introduction to the Idea of Christianity* (New York: Crossroad, 1999), 143.

2. Hans Urs von Balthasar, *Explorations in Theology*, vol. 3, *Creator Spirit* (San Francisco: Ignatius, 1993), 154.

Chapter 8—pages 115–28

1. John P. Meier, "Jesus," from *The New Jerome Biblical Commentary*, ed. Raymond Brown et al (Englewood Cliffs, NJ: Prentice Hall, 1990), 78:17.

2. Pope Francis, "Like Blowing on Embers," September 21, 2013, http://www.news.va/en/news/like-blowing-on-the-embers.

3. David W. Fagerberg, *Theologia Prima: What Is Liturgical Theology?* (Chicago: Hillenbrand, 2004), 31.

4. Marty Haugen's song lyrics describe this clearly: "We remember how you loved us . . . and still we celebrate that you are with us here . . . we remember, we celebrate, we believe." From that celebration, we then act.

5. Fagerberg, 41–42.

6. Some memories are more easily recalled than others. They "stick" at varying rates. Wayne D. Hoyer and Deborah J. MacInnis, *Consumer Behavior*, 3rd ed. (Boston: Houghton Mifflin, 2008), 172–95.

7. Inner assent is not to be diminished simply to an emotional experience. The pathways to encounter may be through an intellectual assent ("I get it!"), through the heart ("I feel it!"), or through the will with an inner sense of rightness of duty, responsibility, and/or commitment ("I will do it!"). See the author's 2013 Academy of Homiletics paper for more about the pathways that bring a believer and a community into an encounter with Jesus Christ. Different pathways have taken the lead in the various historical eras of preaching.

8. See Dan Ariely, *Predictably Irrational: The Hidden Forces That Shape Our Decisions* (New York: Harper, 2009).

9. Hoyer and MacInnis, 135.

10. Marketers call that "positioning"—the creating of an identity or mental picture that is readily recalled from memory.

11. Second Vatican Council, *Unitatis Redintegratio* (*Decree on Ecumenism*, 1964).

12. John Paul II, *Sollicitudo Rei Socialis* (Encyclical Letter for the twentieth anniversary of *Populorum Progressio*), http://www.vatican.va/holy_father/john_paul_ii/encyclicals/documents/hf_jp-ii_enc_30121987_sollicitudo-rei-socialis_en.html.

13. Yves Congar, *I Believe in the Holy Spirit* (New York: Crossroad, 2004), 272.

14. If the emotional blocks do not respond to prayer for healing, seek professional help, or do both.

15. Much more depth on this topic can be found by reading Douglas Stone, Bruce Patton, and Sheila Heen, *Difficult Conversations: How to Discuss What Matters Most* (New York: Penguin, 1999), 118.

16. From the collaborative study between The Emerging Models Project and the Center for Applied Research in the Apostolate (CARA) at http://emergingmodels.org/final-report-executive-summary/; "One of the most surprising aspects of the results [of the study of parishes] so far has been how positive Mass attending Catholics are in their evaluations of their parish." http://nineteensixty-four.blogspot.com/2012/06/parish-drive-by.html.

17. See Karla J. Bellinger, "To Be Young and Catholic in the U.S.: Finding Ways to Let the Holy Spirit Evangelize for You," *Momentum* (Nov/Dec 2013).

18. In the thesis *Are You Talking to Me?* 93% of the youth who both attended Mass regularly and provided feedback offered their comments to those preachers whose homilies they rated as above average or excellent (p. 150). In the *Catechesis in Preaching Research Initiative* 97% of those who work as catechetical leaders in a parish responded "rarely" or "never" to the descriptor: "I give feedback to a homilist when his preaching is poor." For more on the interrelationships between catechetical leaders and homilists, see table 2 in Karla J. Bellinger, "The Elephant in the Room: Catechetical Leaders Speak about the Sunday Homily," *Catechetical Leader* 25, no. 2 (March 2014): 18–24.

19. Pope Francis, Homily for Chrism Mass, 2013, http://www.vatican.va/holy _father/francesco/homilies/2013/documents/papa-francesco_20130328 _messa-crismale_en.html.

20. Dean R. Hoge, *The First Five Years of the Priesthood* (Collegeville, MN: Liturgical Press, 2002), 23.

21. In consulting with homilists about their preaching, we not only videotape and then observe the homily, but we run a parallel video of the parishioners to observe moments of responsiveness and disconnect. It is enlightening.

22. O'Brien Atkinson, *How to Make Us Want Your Sermon: By a Listener* (New York: Joseph F. Wagner, 1942), 173.

23. Chris Chatteris, SJ, "Preaching in a Vacuum," *America*, May 2009.

24. Have your youth group sit in the front pew for a month and see what happens.

25. The National Leadership Roundtable on Church Management is taking the lead in integrating lay leadership with bishops and pastors to strengthen church management. See their valuable contribution and initiatives at http://www .theleadershiproundtable.org/. Rebuilt also has a valuable section (chapter 11) on making every member a minister to lighten the load on the clergy; this vision of parish ownership is laid out by Michael White and Tom Corcoran, *Rebuilt: The Story of a Catholic Parish* (Notre Dame, IN: Ave Maria, 2013).

Chapter 9—pages 129–44

1. Karl Rahner, SJ, *Servants of the Lord*, 20: "In the midst of all this history, at a thousand different times and places, in a thousand forms, the one thing occurs which produces and sustains it all: the silent coming of God."

2. Before sending off the story at the beginning of this chapter, I had to make sure that it was accurate. So after Mass, I snagged the altar server's dad as he headed to the basement for the Scout banquet. "Does [X] believe in miracles?" I asked. "Oh, yes!" he beamed. I told him about the radiance that I had seen in his son's demeanor last Sunday. He hustled down the stairs. "Not only that," he shot back over his head, "he *is* a miracle." (This story was originally published as the opening of Karla J. Bellinger, "My Heart Burns within Me: Sunday Preaching and the Catechesis of Young People" in *Catechetical Leader*, May 2013.)

3. John Paul II, message for the XXXII World Day of Prayer for Vocations, October 18, 1994: "This is what is needed: a Church for young people, which will know how to speak to their heart and enkindle, comfort, and inspire enthusiasm in it with the joy of the Gospel and the strength of the Eucharist; a Church which will know how to invite and to welcome the person who seeks a purpose for

which to commit his whole existence; a Church which is not afraid to require much, after having given much; which does not fear asking from young people the effort of a noble and authentic adventure, such as that of the following of the Gospel."

4. Van Thanh Nguyen, "Preaching Across Cultures: Response to a Pastoral Need in the Church Today," *Seminary Journal* 16 (2010), 18.

5. Work fatigue: 38 percent of employed Americans said they had experienced "low levels of energy, poor sleep, or a feeling of fatigue" during the past two weeks, "Fatigue in the Workplace Is Common and Costly"; http://www .medicalnewstoday.com/releases/60732.php.

6. The Bishops Committee on Priestly Life and Ministry, *Fulfilled in Your Hearing: The Homily in the Sunday Assembly* (Washington, DC: United States Catholic Conference, 1982), 38. The study of this timeless document would be a good next step after reading this book. Other suggestions for further group study can be found in the back of this book.

7. Chris Chatteris, SJ, "Preaching in a Vacuum," *America*, May 25, 2009, http:// www.america magazine.org/content/article.cfm?article_id=11679.

8. David J. Shea, "Unmet Needs in Catholic Preaching: A Project of the Archdiocese of Cincinnati," *Seminary Journal* 16, no. 2 (Fall 2010), 33.

9. Richard C. Stern, "Preaching as Listening: Good Preachers Listen First," *Church* 15, no. 4 (Winter 1999), 24.

10. For a description of a highly painful feedback exchange, see the first of the comments at: http://americamagazine.org/issue/699/article/preaching-vacuum.

11. *Fulfilled in Your Hearing* also recommended staff and clergy homily preparation groups, see p. 38.

12. Richard John Neuhaus, a Lutheran minister turned Catholic priest, said, "It is only human that low expectations and low execution go together; homiletically speaking, priests are under little pressure. Ten minutes of more-or-less impromptu 'reflections' vaguely related to the Scripture lessons of the day, combined with a little story or personal anecdote, is 'good enough'. . . . As one priest friend half-jokingly remarked in defense of homiletical mediocrity, 'We must be careful not to raise their expectations.'" Richard John Neuhaus, "Low Expectations and Catholic Preaching," *First Things: A Monthly Journal of Religion and Public Life*, April 1, 2004.

13. That makes me a tougher preaching coach.

14. What about the 18 percent who are willing to admit (on paper) that they are not above average? That seems like a receptive group for preaching interaction, if they would be willing to admit that and ask for help. If one out of three preachers needs help with basic oral communication skills, this is not a giant hurdle; some honesty from parishioners could make a helpful difference here.

15. John Paul II, *Catechesi Tradendae* (Apostolic Exhortation on Catechesis in our Time), no. 5; John Cavadini, "Preaching and Catechesis: Mending the Rift between Scripture and Doctrine," in *We Preach Christ Crucified*, ed. Michael E. Connors (Collegeville, MN: Liturgical Press, 2014), 66–82.

16. For updates into research initiatives for the evaluation of encounter, see http://www.thecenterforpep.com/our-work/research-initiatives/.

17. For samples of these tools for parish use, see http://www.thecenterforpep .com/our-work/.

18. Theologically, this is one of the weaknesses of our current cultural mind-set—if there is no test at the end of life from the divine Test-Giver, then, "meh . . . what does it really matter how I live my life?" Earlier generations did not have such a presumption that God would give them a "free pass."

19. In the movie *Chariots of Fire*, the dons of Oxford felt that the use of a professional coach to train runners was plebian, beneath their dignity; Harold Abrams assured the august gentlemen that the future would go with him. We could only hope for the same effort poured into homiletics training as has been poured into athletic training since 1924.

20. For an in-depth discussion of the evaluative questions, "What makes for excellence in preaching?" and "How do we know when we've gotten there?" see Karla J. Bellinger, "And . . . How's It Going?"

21. The premise of the *Talent Code* is that those who have grown expert in their abilities have learned to practice deeply; see part one of Daniel Coyle, *Talent Code: Greatness Isn't Born, It's Grown* (New York: Random House, 2009). Modeling of effective preaching skills at a young listener age also makes a difference. Good preachers often sat at the foot of good preachers as children (for example, Martin Luther King, Jr., had a fine role model in his preacher-father); thus preaching can be both caught and taught.

22. Perhaps one reason that the Sunday homily has fallen through the Catholic cracks is because it does not fit neatly into any one particular sphere of influence? In Protestant denominations it has a more prominent institutional presence.

23. The publishing of the 2012 preaching statement, *Preaching the Mystery of Faith*, a collaboration seven national offices, was a healthy first step in highlighting the value of the Sunday homily for the new evangelization.

24. Paul VI, *Presbyterorum Ordinis* (Encyclical Letter on the *Decree on the Ministry and Life of Priests*, 1965), no. 4.

25. The one exception is the Marten family who support our country's two Catholic homiletics centers; many thanks to (the late) John Sr. and Virginia for their sense of vision.

Bibliography

Atkinson, O'Brien. *How to Make Us Want Your Sermon: By a Listener.* New York: Joseph F. Wagner, 1942.

Bellinger, Karla J. "Are You Talking to Me? A Study of Young Listeners' Connection with Catholic Sunday Preaching." DMin thesis, Aquinas Institute of Theology, 2012.

———. "And . . . How's It Going? Preaching Itself as Difficult Conversation." Paper presented at the Academy of Homiletics, Louisville, KY, December 2013.

———. *The Catechesis in Preaching Research Initiative Report,* a collaboration with the National Conference for Catechetical Leadership (NCCL), March 2014. http://www.thecenterforpep.com/our-work/research-initiatives/the-catechesis-in-preaching-initiative.

———. "The Elephant in the Room: Catechetical Leaders Speak about the Sunday Homily," *Catechetical Leader* 25, no. 2 (March 2014): 18–24.

———. "My Heart Burns Within Me: Sunday Preaching and the Catechesis of Young People," *Catechetical Leader* 24, no. 3 (May 2013): 20–23.

———. "To Be Young and Catholic in the United States: Finding Ways to Let the Holy Spirit Evangelize for You," *Momentum,* Nov/Dec 2013, 11–14.

———. "Vatican II: Connecting with the Next Generation," *AIM: Liturgy Resources,* Fall 2013, 10–13.

Benedict XVI. *Verbum Domini* [Post-Synodal Apostolic Exhortation, 2010]. Vatican. http://www.vatican.va/holy_father/benedict_xvi/apost_exhortations/documents/hf_ben-xvi_exh_20100930_verbum-domini_en.html.

Bokenkotter, Thomas. *A Concise History of the Catholic Church.* New York: Doubleday, 1990.

Carrell, Lori. *The Great American Sermon Survey.* Wheaton, IL: Mainstay Church Resources, 2000.

———. *Preaching that Matters: Reflective Practices for Transforming Sermons.* Herndon, VA: Alban, 2013.

Cialdini, Robert B. *Influence: The Psychology of Persuasion*. New York: HarperCollins Business Essentials, 2007.

Center for Applied Research in the Apostolate (CARA). "The Class of 2011: Survey of Ordinands to the Priesthood." CARA. http://www.usccb.org/beliefs-and-teachings/vocations/ordination-class/upload/ordination-class-2011-report.pdf.

———. "The Impact of Religious Switching and Secularization on the Estimated Size of the U.S. Adult Catholic Population." CARA. http://cara.georgetown.edu/rel022 808.pdf.

———. "Priests in the United States: Satisfaction, Work Load and Support Structures." CARA. http://www.stmsfc.org/WORKLOADFORPRIESTS%201%2024%2010.pdf.

———. "Self-reported Mass Attendance of U.S. Catholics Unchanged during Last Five Years." CARA. http://cara.georgetown.edu/AttendPR.pdf.

Chatteris, Chris, SJ. "Preaching in a Vacuum." *America* (May 25, 2009). http://www.americamagazine.org/content/article.cfm?article_id=11679.

Chauvet, Louis-Marie. *The Sacraments: The Word of God at the Mercy of the Body*. Collegeville, MN: Liturgical Press, 2001.

Congar, Yves. *I Believe in the Holy Spirit*. New York: Crossroad Publishing, 2004.

Dean, Kenda. *Almost Christian: What the Faith of Our Teenagers Is Telling the American Church*. New York: Oxford University Press, 2010.

———. "Preaching to Youth." in *The New Interpreter's Handbook of Preaching*, edited by Paul Scott Wilson, Jana Childers, Cleophus J. LaRue, and John M. Rottman. Nashville, TN: Abingdon Press, 2008.

DeLeers, Stephen. *Written Text becomes Living Word: The Vision and Practice of Sunday Preaching*. Collegeville, MN: Liturgical Press, 2004.

Dolan, Timothy. *Priests for the Third Millennium*. Huntington, IN: Our Sunday Visitor, 2000.

Dulles, Avery. *Models of the Church*. New York: Random House, 2000.

———. "Vatican II: The Myth and the Reality," *America*, February 24, 2003.

Edwards, Otis Carl, Jr. *A History of Preaching*. Nashville, TN: Abingdon Press, 2004.

Fagerberg, David. *Theologia Prima: What Is Liturgical Theology?* Chicago: Hillenbrand Books, 2004.

Francis, Pope. "A Big Heart Open to God," interview with Antonio Spadaro, SJ, in *America,* September 30, 2013, http://www.americamagazine.org/popeinterview.

———. "Like Blowing on Embers," http://www.news.va/en/news/like-blowing-on-the-embers.

————. "Homily for Chrism Mass, 2013." http://www.vatican.va/holy_father /francesco/homilies/2013/documents/papa-francesco_20130328_messa crismale_en.html.

Gladwell, Malcolm. *The Tipping Point: How Little Things Can Make a Big Differ- ence.* New York: Little, Brown and Company, 2002.

Graves, Mike. *The Fully Alive Preacher.* Louisville: Westminster John Knox Press, 2006.

Gautier, Mary, Paul M. Perl, and Stephen J. Fichter. *Same Call, Different Men: The Evolution of the Priesthood Since Vatican II.* Collegeville, MN: Liturgical Press, 2012.

Harris, Daniel E. *We Speak the Word of the Lord: A Practical Plan for More Effective Preaching.* Chicago: ACTA, 2001.

Heath, Chip and Dan Heath. *Made to Stick: Why Some Ideas Succeed and Others Die.* New York: Random House, 2007.

Hilkert, Mary Catherine. *Naming Grace: Preaching and the Sacramental Imagination.* New York: Continuum, 1998.

Hoge, Dean R. *The First Five Years of the Priesthood.* Collegeville, MN: Liturgical Press, 2002.

Hoyer, Wayne D. and Deborah J. MacInnis. *Consumer Behavior,* 3rd ed. Boston: Houghton Mifflin, 2008.

Jedin, Hubert. *A History of the Council of Trent,* vol. 1. London: Thomas Nelson and Sons, 1957.

John XXIII. "Address on the Occasion of the Solemn Opening of the Most Holy Council." http://www.vatican.va/holy_father/john_xxiii/speeches /1962/index_en.htm.

John Paul II, *Pastores Dabo Vobis* [Post-synodal Apostolic Exhortation, On the Formation of Priests, 1992].

————. *Sollicitudo Rei Socialis* [Encyclical Letter For the Twentieth Anni- versary Of Populorum Progressio] http://www.vatican.va/holy_father /john_paul_ii/encyclicals/documents/hf_jp-ii_enc_30121987_sollicitudo -rei-socialis_en.html.

Jungmann, Josef, SJ, "The Defeat of Teutonic Arianism and the Revolution in Religious Culture in the Early Middle Ages," *Pastoral Liturgy,* New York, 1962, 1-101.

Lovrick, Peter. "A Pedagogical Model for Homiletics at St. Augustine's Semi- nary: They Must Increase, and I Must Decrease." DMin thesis, Aquinas Insti- tute, 2009.

Malina, Bruce. *The New Testament World: Insights from Cultural Anthropology,* 3rd ed. Louisville: Westminster John Knox Press, 2001.

McCarty, Robert J. "Young People Are Listening! Preaching and Liturgy with Youth." *Seminary Journal* 13 (2007): 24–27.

McCrabb, Donald R. "Improving Preaching through Feedback." *Seminary Journal* 16, Fall 2010.

Meier, John P. "Jesus," from *The New Jerome Biblical Commentary*, ed. Raymond Brown et al. Englewood Cliffs, NJ: Prentice Hall, 1990.

Murphy-O'Connor, Jerome. *Paul: A Critical Life*. New York: Oxford University Press, 1996.

Neuhaus, Richard John. "Low Expectations and Catholic Preaching." *First Things: A Monthly Journal of Religion and Public Life,* April 2004.

Nguyen, van Thanh. "Preaching Across Cultures: Response to a Pastoral Need in the Church Today." *Seminary Journal* 16 (2010).

Old, Hughes Oliphant. *The Reading and Preaching of the Scriptures in the Worship of the Christian Church: the Medieval Period*. Grand Rapids, MI: Wm. B. Eerdmans, 1999.

Paul VI. *Apostolicam Actuositatem* [Encyclical Letter, Decree on the Apostolate of Lay People, 1965]. Northport, NY: Costello Publishing Co., 1996.

———. *Dei Verbum* [Vatican II Document, *Dogmatic Constitution on Divine Revelation*, 1965]. Washington, DC: United States Catholic Conference, 2000.

———. *Evangelii Nuntiandi* [Apostolic Letter, *On Evangelization in the Modern World*, 1975]. Washington, DC: United States Catholic Conference, 2000.

———. *Gaudium et Spes* [Vatican II document, *On the Church in the Modern World,* 1965]. Washington, DC: United States Catholic Conference, 2000.

———. *Lumen Gentium* [Vatican II document, *Dogmatic Constitution on the Church*, 1964]. Washington, DC: United States Catholic Conference, 2000.

———. *Presbyterorum Ordinis* [Encyclical Letter, *The Decree on the Ministry and Life of Priests,* 1965]. Northport, NY: Costello Publishing Co., 1996.

———. *Sacrosanctum Concilium* [Vatican II Document, *Constitution on the Sacred Liturgy*, 1963]. Washington, DC: United States Catholic Conference, 2000.

———. *Unitatis Redintegratio* [Vatican II Document, *Decree on Ecumenism*, 1964]. Northport, NY: Costello Publishing Co., 1996.

Pew Forum on Religion and Public Life. "Faith in Flux: Changes in Religious Affiliation in the U.S." The Pew Research Center. http://pewforum.org/Faith-in-Flux3.aspx.

———. "Catholics Share Bishops Concerns about Religious Liberty." The Pew Research Center, November 2012. http://www.pewforum.org/Politics and -Elections/Catholics-Share-Bishops-Concerns-about-Religious-Liberty .aspx#leaders.

———. "'Nones' on the Rise." The Pew Research Center, October 2012. http://www.pewforum.org/2012/10/09/nones-on-the-rise/.

————. "U.S. Religious Knowledge Survey." The Pew Research Center. http://pewforum.org/U-S-Religious-Knowledge-Survey-Who-Knows-What-About-Religion.aspx.

Pius X, *Vehementer Nos* [Papal Encyclical, *On the French Law of Separation*, 1906].

————. *The 1917 Pio-Benedictine Code of Canon Law: In English Translation*. San Francisco: Ignatius, 2001.

Rahner, Karl. *Foundations of Christian Faith: An Introduction to the Idea of Christianity*. New York: Crossroad, 1999.

Ramshaw, Gail. *Reviving Sacred Speech: The Meaning of Liturgical Language*. Akron, OH: OSL Publications, 2000.

Resner, Andre. "Ethos" in *The New Interpreter's Handbook of Preaching*, ed. Paul Scott Wilson et al., 350. Nashville, TN: Abingdon Press, 2008.

Reynolds, Sean. "Forming Young Disciples: Are We Asking the Right Questions?" *Sourcebook on Adolescent Catechesis,* vol. 2, ch. 8. National Initiative for Adolescent Catechesis, 2009. http://adolescentcatechesis.org/wp-content/uploads/2009/08/Reynolds-Asking-Right-Questions.pdf?phpMyAdmin=42127c7fd043c66a3708134c9f5c61ca [accessed November 12, 2010].

Ries, Al and Jack Trout. *Positioning: The Battle for Your Mind: How to be Seen and Heard in the Overcrowded Marketplace*. New York: McGraw-Hill, 2001.

Robinson, Denis, OSB. "With One Voice: A Program for Parishes." *Seminary Journal* 16 (2010): 21–25.

Schmitt, Katherine. "Effective Preaching: What Catholics Want—A Project of the NCEA Seminary Department." *Seminary Journal* 16 (2010): 26–30.

Shea, David J. "Self-Understanding in Catholic Preaching: How the Identity of the Priest Shapes His Approach to Preaching." DMin thesis, Aquinas Institute, 2006.

————. "Unmet Needs in Catholic Preaching: A Project of the Archdiocese of Cincinnati." *Seminary Journal* 16 (2010): 33–41.

Smith, Christian. *Soul Searching: The Religious and Spiritual Lives of American Teenagers*. New York: Oxford University Press, 2005.

Stone, Douglas, Bruce Patton, and Sheila Heen. *Difficult Conversations: How to Discuss What Matters Most*. New York: Penguin, 1999.

Tisdale, Leonora Tubbs. *Preaching as Local Theology and Folk Art*. Minneapolis: Fortress Press, 1997.

Torrens, James S. "Lessons from Evangelicals: An Interview with Manuel Flores." *America,* July 19, 2004. http://www.americamagazine.org/content/article.cfm?article_id=3679.

United States Conference of Catholic Bishops. *The Basic Plan for the Ongoing Formation of Priests*. Washington, DC: United States Catholic Conference, 2001.

————. *Fulfilled in Your Hearing: The Homily in the Sunday Assembly.* Washington, D.C.: United States Catholic Conference, 1982.

————. *Program of Priestly Formation,* 5th ed. Washington, DC: United States Catholic Conference, 2006.

————. *Preaching the Mystery of Faith: The Sunday Homily.* Washington, DC: United States Catholic Conference, 2012.

————. *Renewing the Vision: A Framework for Catholic Youth Ministry.* Washington, DC: United States Catholic Conference, 1997.

Untener, Ken. *Preaching Better: Practical Suggestions for Homilists.* New York: Paulist, 1999.

Voelz, Richard W. "Preaching, Adolescent Youth, and the Turn to the 'Other': An Agenda for Homiletics." Paper presented at the Academy of Homiletics, Minneapolis, MN, December 2007.

Von Balthasar, Hans Urs. *Creator Spirit.* Vol. 3 of *Explorations in Theology.* San Francisco: Ignatius, 1993.

White, Michael and Tom Corcoran. *Rebuilt: The Story of a Catholic Parish.* Notre Dame, IN: Ave Maria, 2013.

Youngs, Deborah. *The Life-Cycle in Western Europe, c. 1300–1500.* New York: Palgrave, 2006.